Animus and Anima
in Fairy Tales

Marie-Louise von Franz, Honorary Patron

**Studies in Jungian Psychology
by Jungian Analysts**

Daryl Sharp, General Editor

ANIMUS AND ANIMA
IN FAIRY TALES

MARIE-LOUISE VON FRANZ
Edited by Daryl Sharp

Library and Archives Canada Cataloguing in Publication

Franz, Marie-Louise von,
Animus and Anima in Fairy Tales / Marie-Louise von Franz

(Studies in Jungian psychology by Jungian analysts ; 100)
Includes bibliographical references and index.

ISBN 9781894574013 (softcover)

1. Fairy Tales-Psychological aspects.
2. Animus (Psychoanalysis) in literature.
3. Anima (Psychoanalysis) in literature.
I. Sharp, Daryl, 1936-. II. Title.
III. Series: Studies in Jungian psychology by Jungian analysts ; 100

GR550.F678 2002   398.2'01'9   C2002-900224-9

INNER CITY BOOKS
21 Milroy Crescent
Toronto, ON M1C 4B6, Canada.
416-927-0355
www.innercitybooks.net / booksales@innercitybooks.net

Honorary Patron: Marie-Louise von Franz.
Publisher and General Editor: Daryl Sharp.
Senior Editor: Victoria B. Cowan.
Office Manager: Scott Milligen.
IT Manager: Sharpconnections.com.
Editorial Assistance: David Sharp, J. Morgan, E. Jefferson.

INNER CITY BOOKS was founded in 1980 to promote the
understanding and practical application of the work of C. G. Jung.

Index by Vicki Cowan.

Printed and bound in Canada by Rapido Livres Books.
Reprinted 2023

CONTENTS

Marie-Louise von Franz, 1915-1998

Marie-Louise von Franz emigrated to Switzerland from Austria with her family in 1918. In 1933, at the age of 18, she attended a lecture by Professor C.G. Jung, then a mature 58. In his talk, Jung referred to a woman he had treated who "lived on the moon." The young Marie-Louise asked timorously if he meant that it was "as if" she lived on the moon. Jung replied, "No, not 'as if,' she *did* live on the moon."

This was von Franz's introduction to the reality of the unconscious. The very next year she began to work with Jung, first in analysis and then as his assistant in translating arcane alchemical texts, and did so until his death in 1961. In 1938 she was granted Swiss citizenship. In 1940 she received her doctorate in classical languages from the University of Zürich. In 1948 she was a co-founder, with Jung, of the C.G. Jung Institute of Zürich. Thereafter she lectured extensively and became internationally known as the doyenne of Jungian analysts, renowned for her work on synchronicity, dreams, alchemy and fairy tales.

Editor's Foreword

During my four years at the C.G. Jung Institute of Zürich (1974-1978), I went to all of Dr. von Franz's lectures and read everything she ever wrote. Some of her seminars had been transcribed and were available in mimeographed form. Several were published by Spring: *Introduction to the Interpretation of Fairy Tales, The Feminine in Fairy Tales, Shadow and Evil in Fairy Tales, Individuation in Fairy Tales.* I found these and others particularly valuable in amplifying the meaning of images that turned up nightly in my dreams. I devoured them and lamented the fact that they were not indexed. But not for long.

Before I found myself on my knees I had been a freelance editor, and so I set about creating indexes for her fairy tale books, as well as for my first love of hers, *The Problem of the Puer Aeternus.* I photocopied my painstaking work and sold it to other students and past graduates. Eventually Spring bought the rights to these indexes and incorporated them in subsequent printings. The benefit to me was twofold: I absorbed von Franz's attitude toward the psyche and I was able to pay my tuition fees.

*

In 1978 I returned to Toronto as a certified Jungian analyst. Thanks to the groundwork laid by the late James M. Shaw and the late Robertson Davies, who had co-founded the Jung Foundation of Ontario in 1970, I soon had a thriving practice. Still, I was restless. I had so much energy I thought I might explode.

For some time I had been trying to interest publishers in my Diploma thesis on Franz Kafka, *The Secret Raven: Conflict and Transformation.* I had high hopes. The 100th anniversary of his birth was coming up, and then the 60th anniversary of his death. But there were no takers. I was frustrated. And then Marion Woodman and the late Fraser Boa, close friends and fellow Zürich graduates, encouraged me to publish it myself. "Why not?" they said. "You have the tools."

7

Well, that was true. I knew what was involved in making and marketing a book. Yes, I thought, why not! Only I did not fancy being a one-shot vanity press, so I invited manuscripts from other analysts. Marion immediately offered her own thesis on obesity and anorexia, *The Owl Was a Baker's Daughter.* Then, on a sunny day in May of 1980, I plucked up my courage and called Dr. von Franz at her home in Küsnacht, not forgetting the six-hour time difference.

"Mr. Sharp?" she said. "In Canada?! Oh, how are you? I have just come in from the garden. It is a wonderful spring for tulips, don't you think?"

I readily agreed.

"Dr. von Franz," I said. "I am starting a publishing house and I'm interested in some of your unpublished seminars. I'm thinking of *Redemption Motifs in Fairy Tales, On Synchronicity and Divination* and *Alchemy: An Introduction to the Symbolism and the Psychology.* I have mimeographed copies."

She said she was very pleased to be asked. What is more, she graciously agreed to be Honorary Patron of Inner City Books. Those three books of hers have sold over 80,000 copies to date.

Periodically I wrote von Franz asking if she had other manuscripts Inner City might publish. My persistence was rewarded in 1996 when she offered *Archetypal Patterns in Fairy Tales* and reprint rights to *Puer Aeternus* and *C.G. Jung: His Myth in Our Time.* Just six months before she died, she gave us another hitherto unpublished fairy tale seminar, *The Cat: A Tale of Feminine Redemption.* Most recently we published a reprint of her *Aurora Consurgens: On the Problem of Opposites in Alchemy.*

*

On the morning of February 17, 1998, I awoke to find an e-mail message from Bob Hinshaw, fellow analyst and publisher of Daimon Books in Einsiedeln, Switzerland: "Sad news from Zürich. Marlus died early this morning. She has been ailing for quite some time and this was surely her deliverance."

The farewell service was scheduled to be held in the Reform Church of Küsnacht on February 26. I am averse to travel, especially to trips across multiple time-zones, and so for a few days I resisted the idea of being there. But in the end I had to go. She was my patron, after all, and the inner urge to publicly honor our association was just too great. And what a joyful occasion it turned out to be: a simple service with heart-felt valedictory addresses and a Schubert concert, followed by a sumptuous buffet and a seemingly endless supply of Swiss wine—all provided for in advance by von Franz herself.

In the midst of all this, I had a sudden realization. This dearly departed old woman, a self-professed thinking type who had often publically confessed her difficulty with her inferior feeling function—to the extent of having to memorize collective expressions of sympathy, congratulations on weddings, etc.—had done *this* for *us*. Well, if that does not betoken an integration of opposites, I don't know what does. I silently thanked her for this *sotto voce* example of the *coniunctio*.

So, in 1998 the world-wide Jungian community lost a great lady, and Inner City lost a beloved patron. But the spirit of Marie-Louise von Franz lives on—in her books, in those she worked with analytically, and in the many thousands of others who have been helped or influenced by her writings. Her legacy will surely be that she appreciated Jung's message and did her utmost to further it. And more, for she was not a mindless devotee of Jung. She made her own mark, put her own inimitable stamp both on Jungian psychology and on those she taught.

*

Appropriately enough, this present book is the 100th title to be published by Inner City. It is based on extensive notes taken by Ms. Cassil Welch, who attended the seminars given in 1953 by Dr. von Franz to the Los Angeles Society of Analytical Psychology. It has been my joyful task to turn these notes into a book, always mindful of von Franz's distinctive voice.

Animus and Anima in Fairy Tales is unique in that it is the only book by a Jungian analyst which deals exclusively with the problem of the contrasexual complexes as it is illuminated by fairy tales. There are of course other commentaries by analysts on the animus and anima—as listed here in a section of the Bibliography—but none that focuses on them *exclusively* in terms of fairy tales. Since Dr. von Franz was the acknowledged expert on the psychological interpretation of fairy tales, this book has a particular value for those interested in the subject.

Meanwhile, we understand from the heirs of her literary estate (Emmanuel Kennedy and the Stiftung für Jung'sche Psychologie) that other unpublished manuscripts (and more by the late Barbara Hannah as well) will be available in the near future. We await them with great anticipation.

Personally, I feel privileged and fortunate indeed to be in a position to keep alive the work and spirit of Marie-Louise von Franz, to the benefit of everyone who strives to become psychologically conscious.

Daryl Sharp

Preface

The animus is a cunning fox who knows how
to hide his footprints with his tail.
—C.G. Jung.

Fairy tales represent something very much removed from human consciousness. I once heard Jung say that if one interprets a fairy tale thoroughly, one must take at least a week's holiday afterward, because it is so difficult.

The difficulty is due to the fact that the fairy tale is based on certain functions of the psyche without any personal material to bridge it. What we have is just the skeleton of the psyche with the skin and flesh removed. Only that remains which is of general human interest. They are absolutely abstract patterns.

In primitive tales there is an element present that has been lost in most of the later ones, namely the element of awe, of terror, of the divine, which early people experienced in meeting the archetypes.

Here we will look at a few of these tales and try to figure out what they can tell us about the psychic functions we call animus, the inner masculine figure in a woman, and anima, the inner feminine figure in a man.

1
Old Rinkrank

In this northern German fairy tale,[1] a king had a daughter. He made a glass mountain and said that only a man who could walk over this mountain could have his daughter. Along comes a man who loves her and wants to marry her. The princess wants to walk over the glass mountain with him. So they start out together, but before long the mountain opens and the girl falls into it; then it closes up again. Inside the glass mountain is an old man with a beard seventeen inches long. He asks her to be his maid. He calls her Mrs. Mansrot (Man's Red) and tells her to call him Old Rinkrank or Red Knight. Every day he disappears through a small window which he reaches by a ladder, and every night he returns with silver and gold which he piles up.

One day she decides to escape. She pulls the window down on Rinkrank's beard, keeping him fastened there until he agrees to let her have the ladder. She returns to the king, who goes and kills Old Rinkrank, taking all the gold and silver. Then the princess marries the man who had asked for her in the beginning.

*

In interpreting fairy tales, it is important to start at the beginning and ask, "Who is lacking to make a complete family?" Generally the element lacking in human form reappears later in another form. Something happens in the flow of the story, and that which was incomplete completes itself. The story starts with an unsatisfactory situation, and then shows how the completion comes about.

"A king has a daughter . . ." If this were an individual case, we

---

[1] [See Grimm Brother, *The Complete Grimm's Fairy Tales,* pp. 796ff.—Ed.]

would assume that it concerns a father complex. Generally the animus in a woman develops out of her experience of the personal father. He puts flesh on the inborn archetype of the father, and that experience becomes her father complex, which manifests both in her attitude toward men in her life and in the functioning of her inner masculinity, which we call the animus.

There is no mother in this story. Still thinking in terms of a personal situation, it is generally true that if a mother figure is lacking there is likely to be weakness and uncertainty on a woman's feminine side. This naturally exposes her to the danger of animus possession.

However, a fairy tale is not case material. "A king" is *not* just the father; it is said specifically that he is a *king*. This represents what happens when archetypes are at home with each other; that is, as processes within the collective unconscious, they are much more basic than personal material, though personal material is based on these processes. So, here a king and princess are at the center of the story.

Fairy tales usually deal with either royal persons or with the lowest, anonymous type of person, like a hunter or an old soldier or a miller. This shows that the material refers to a superpersonal or subpersonal level. The king is the outstanding person in a given society.

Traditionally the figure of a king represents God on earth; he is an incarnation of God. However, in fairy tales and myths, kings are usually incomplete, perhaps blind or infirm, needing rejuvenation, the water of life. The king actually represents that idea of the Self, the regulating center of the psyche, that has become a representation of the collective attitude.

For instance, in terms of the Western world today, Christ may be looked upon as the central idea of a political state. But it is incomplete; it represents only the dominant attitude of the collective culture. This center can become old and obsolete. This is the moment when renewal must take place, opening up the real meaning, the experience, that underlies all religious systems. Hundreds of fairy tales depict this process, telling how it comes about.

Here the king makes a sort of glass trap, not for his daughter but for her suitors. He represents an aspect of the collective attitude which has become very wrong, incomplete. Apparently the queen has died; we aren't told that for sure, but in any case the corresponding feminine factor linked with the king—the feeling or Eros aspect of the dominant ruling attitude—is gone.

Every system—social, political or religious—is associated with a certain feeling attitude. For example, the birth of Christianity as the old Roman Empire was declining meant a change of attitude toward Logos, toward marriage, toward slaves, toward the system. Thus, always, all ruling attitudes are accompanied by some feeling attitude. If the queen is absent, it means there is no longer any Eros in the old ruling system. That is why the whole weight of the story goes on the daughter. The renewal of the kingdom, the necessary balance provided by the feminine, comes through the princess.

The glass trap the king makes suggests the mother substitute, since mountains have long been worshipped as holy, the home of mother goddesses. Jung says that mountains may also represent the outstanding personality, the Self.[2] This is so because mountains are a sure point of orientation to one who is on the plain. Certain Church Fathers have been referred to as mountains looming above the plain. Going up, or climbing a mountain is a symbol of becoming more conscious.

The mountain is a heap of earth or stones thrown up by a

---

[2] [See "The Philosophical Tree," *Alchemical Studies,* CW 13, par. 407. (CW refers throughout to *The Collected Works of C.G. Jung)*—Ed.]

volcanic explosion, that is, the throwing up of the insides of the earth. The process of individuation, becoming conscious of who you were meant to be, involves climbing over one's worst, most resistant areas, this earthly mass. By going up the mountain, one becomes the mountain. The ego climbs this mass of material which we find inside ourselves. That is why the mountain can also represent the mother.

In our story the mountain opens like a cup and the girl is caught in it, showing that the feminine aspect is trapped in matter. But the mountain is of glass, and it is not dark. There are other tales where the heroine is imprisoned in a glass coffin.[3] This means being completely cut off, emotionally as well as intellectually. One is *completely* cut off in the isolating prison. In the glass prison one can look out, one has a complete view, but one is still cut off. Glass is also an insulating material, so here the glass mountain alludes to being cut off from the emotional, feeling life. Glassy people are stiff—you can make contact intellectually, but there is no heart in them, no feeling contact.

Thus the king is trying to cut off the feeling contact between the princess and her suitor. He wants to stop life, so that there will be no future king to replace him. Every ruling system has the tendency to resist and petrify the flow of new life.

The many instinctive patterns which higher animals have get into conflict. Man is the only being on this planet who can rule his instincts. That is what consciousness was given to him for. Think of the lemmings in Norway who migrate in huge numbers, probably so that by changing places they will not destroy the land completely and will continue to have food. But if they are headed toward the sea, they cannot change their route but continue until they are all drowned in following this driving instinct.

---

[3] [See, for instance, "The Glass Coffin," in *The Complete Grimm's Fairy Tales,* pp. 672ff.—Ed.]

This is a destructive aspect of instinctive nature, and only consciousness can achieve control over such a mechanism.

Now, it also belongs to the structure of consciousness to become one-sided. This is connected with will power. There is always the danger of becoming cut off from the instincts, becoming unbalanced and destructive, going completely against nature. This is a typical tendency of consciousness, to persevere in a course of action, even though after a while what was once an excellent attitude and a good remedy eventually becomes self-defeating. You see this in the troubles that commonly beset people in the middle of life, but in smaller ways the need for a change of values is constantly present.

In our tale the trick of the old king backfires, for it is the *daughter*, not the suitor, who falls into the trap. The future son-in-law represents that being who is destined to become king. Therefore he represents the germ of a new attitude in the unconscious. Here he is only a catalytic agent, since we are told nothing else about him. Since the masculine element is so vague, and the princess-daughter is more fully characterized—her fate being central—we know that this is probably a story about the animus.

The girl wants to help her future husband go over the mountain, and through that she falls into the trap. We often see that people are caught in a complex, but it is not manifest. The trouble in the story starts only in a crucial moment, namely where she has a chance to get out of the complex. Before this, she seems to be free. It is only when the man wants to marry her that she falls into her father complex.

Thus, *a person with a neurosis has it because the chance of getting out of the complex is being offered.* If such people miss the chance to get out of it when the time is right, then catastrophe comes, sickness and so on. Stories of an encounter with a dragon address this experience; if you face the dragon and win, you gain the treasure. Here the girl can marry, the king can retire, etc., but instead of this she falls into the mountain, the trap. It is not the young man who falls in.

When she falls into the mountain, she finds the old man with a beard. One has the feeling that this old man doesn't earn the silver and gold in an honorable way. He treats the girl as his wife, giving her the name of a married woman, but it is not the same as his name. And she must work for him.

The beard plays an enormous role in fairy tales. You know the story of Bluebeard, who killed his wives. Now he is a wonderful image of the destructive, murderous animus! There is also the tale of King Thrushbeard, which illustrates the transformation of the negative into the positive animus.[4] Here the princess imprisons Old Rinkrank by pulling the window down on his beard.

Hair in general is symbolically significant, but the meaning varies according to the part of the body on which it grows. On the head it generally represents involuntary, unconscious thoughts and fantasies; that is why, in primitive societies, hair has *mana*.[5] Sometimes we can influence our environment much more by our unconscious assumptions than by our conscious thoughts. That is why hair—the spiritual power of our unconscious thoughts—is so important. Delilah destroyed Sampson's soul, castrated him psychologically, by cutting off his hair, his creative thoughts and ideas. There are African tribes where the boys must collect sticks and shells to put in their hair; it is their initiation into adulthood. Then they can marry. In designing their headdress they build up a spiritual philosophy, which they literally wear *on* their heads.

The hair growing on different parts of the body is reminiscent

---

[4] [See ibid., pp. 244ff.—Ed.]

[5] *[Mana* is a Melanesian word referring to a bewitching or numinous quaity in gods or sacred objects.—Ed.]

of our animal nature; it is the remains of the fur we have lost.

So what is the beard? It is the terrific flow of unconscious talk, blind talk, that animus-possessed women are given to. It flows out of their mouth, a lot of trash and a lot of pearls, but they are unconscious of both the trash and the pearls.

In "Old Rinkrank" the girl pins down the beard. This is a common motif in ghost stories, where if one can nail or pin down the ghost it disappears entirely, or proves to be but a bit of straw or something similarly worthless. That is what we do in active imagination—make conscious what is disturbing us or has too much emotional weight. We ask, "Do *I* really believe that?" and so on. When one is possessed by the animus, one has a holy conviction about one's assumptions. But one must ask, "Is that what I *really* believe?" One must pin down the flow.

Who is the old man in the mountain? We assume he is an animus figure, but that is not saying much. We have said that the king represents a collective ruling attitude. So then, who is this being in the mountain, this robber, the old red knight? It is not said that the king put him there. If it were a personal story, we could say that behind the king is the archaic figure of the old man. But we must look at the problem on a collective level.

There is the "red" in his name, and good reason for associating him with another "Red Beard" story that deals with Wotan asleep in the German soul. We can say that this is an older image of God, farther back than the king.

When a ruling figure, a ruling idea, disappears, what usually appears next is an older image of God. You can observe this in the whole current of religious history. When the Greek gods lost their *mana,* the gods who then appeared were more archaic, from the pre-Greek period. But it is not a pure regression—they contain the germ of a new, higher level. Alchemy reappeared on a higher level as the science of chemistry.

The old man in the mountain is a more primitive, pagan image of the German god who reappears. This old demon is gathering values (gold and silver) so that there are no values left in consciousness. This constitutes a very dangerous situation. It is not thought that he should become the secret ruler of the country, for he is killed; the regressive aspect has to be killed, as he is in the end by the king. It is not the daughter who kills him—she leaves it to the king to do that. It is her task only to *escape*. It is the duty of the king, who has attracted this old devil by his attitude, to kill the old man in the mountain.

Women cannot fight the animus by *killing* him—they can only *catch* him by pinning him by the beard so they can then escape. The male hero in myths fights, overcomes, conquers the monster. The feminine follows the path of individuation by suffering and escaping. It is enough if a woman can walk out into the human situation, rebuild human relatedness, relationship.

The king kills Old Rinkrank—as the opposites kill each other. The unconscious creates the conflict, makes two out of one. If you can keep out of it, taking neither this stand nor that, you can escape the evils of conflict. The princess suffers, and then she walks out of it. The only effort she makes is to pin down the old man's beard. She turns him into a helpful servant who provides the way out—the ladder.

In Siberia they talk of a ghost world where the gods lived, but we have lost it. There is now only a cord-ladder with knots in it that makes the connection between the ghost world and our world, and only the shaman or medicine man can cross into the other world. He climbs by means of the knots. This cord or ladder is what we build up every day in analysis, until we experience the feeling, "Ah, now I am connected." The emotional entanglements and conflicts are the knots.

The oldest writings and calculations used cords with knots.

The cord is the meaning, the connection. We see the "connecting links."

The demon Rinkrank provides the princess with a meaning, connection. If a woman hasn't gone through the experience of being trapped by the demon animus, she has only unconscious thoughts. It is the demon who provides her with the ladder to escape. What was negative becomes positive.

We must not forget that fairy tales deal with archetypes, and archetypes cannot be killed. But the tale means that in this particular constellation, the negative aspect disappears. The devil will always appear again, but it will be in another form or constellation; this particular problem will not reappear.

*

There is always a fairy tale level going on in life. Then myths develop out of it, and these sink into fairy tales again.

The princess falling into the mountain is falling into mother, and there she is reborn. Red Knight is there—the passion is inside the mountain. The mother is represented not by a human being but by a mountain. When something is personified as a human being it can be integrated. That which is represented as a mountain enclosing a person means she cannot integrate it but can only relate to it. The positive thing here is that the values are rescued— in the end the gold and silver are possessed by the bride and groom. Here we see that the princess acquires her physical reality by falling into the mountain.

Often in fairy tales the negative hero is called the Red Knight. This shows that there is an emotional link between the girl and the demon. Inside the mountain both their names contain the word "red." Her name, Man's Red, shows a combination of the masculine and passion. Rinkrank, the Red Knight, gives her the name whereby she can realize who she really is.

The great problem of the animus is that when a woman is unconscious of her animus, it links up with her emotional side and she becomes the proverbial "bull in the china shop"—she can develop a masculine mind and look at herself more objectively, but her feminine feeling nature is pressed down and melds with the animus. This causes many tragedies in life, particularly in the realm of relationship.

In our tale the old king does everything to prevent the renewal with his right hand, and everything to help the renewal with his left. Women are always spinning plots to catch someone, and then fall into their own trap. But men play with the anima and she takes the key when they aren't looking!

The fact that the girl goes through the transformation process of suffering, and takes action in pinning down Rinkrank's beard, causes a transformation in him, so that he helps her.

The killing of the evil old man by the king is comparable to the "Christian habit," in the sense of a killing attitude toward life. The demon in the mountain is like the Germanic Wotan as a seed of new life—but the Germans did not use in a positive way the libido that was released.

Communism and the conventional Christian attitude are quite close to each other. The smart thing for us to do is to walk away from them both and let them kill each other. That is how a conflict is always overcome—by walking out of it. In a conflict, the two sides become so close to each other that they use the same weapons. The process of individuation is furthered precisely by not taking part in the battle but rather walking out of it. The two sides hate each other because they are so similar, and they use the same methods. That is why the fairy tale has the king and not the princess kill the demon, and the king will naturally leave the throne, the gold and silver—the "values"—to the princess and her husband.

Regarding Rinkrank being a robber, it is one of the activities of the animus life of a woman to steal, to suck life from other people. Such a woman becomes a vampire because she has no life in herself. But she needs life and so must take it where she finds it. The negative devil-animus kills every feminine aspect in life.

2
The Magic Horse

This Turkestan tale tells the following story.[6]

There was once a king who had a beautiful daughter. When she was grown up, he devised a clever trick to test her suitors. He fed a flea until it grew as big as a camel. Then he killed and skinned it, and announced that the man who could guess to whom or what the skin belonged shall have his daughter.

One day his slave, who had gone to fetch water from the pool, exclaimed to himself, "Oh, they are fools not to guess that this is the skin of a flea."

He was overheard by the Div, the evil spirit who lived in the pool. This Div changed himself into a beggar and went to court and told the king, "I know what that skin is—it is the skin of a flea."

The king was very unhappy, but had to keep his promise to give the beggar his daughter. He didn't want to, but the Div threw his cap up in the air and a black fog covered the sky like night. This frightened the king, so that he gave up his daughter. Then the Div threw the cap on the ground, and there was light over the land again.

The daughter was naturally very sad and miserable, and she went out alone to the king's stable to cry. A little horse or pony in the stable spoke to her: "Take me with you, and also bring a pink (the name of a flower), a comb, a mirror and some salt."

The princess obtains these items and begins the journey with the Div, taking along the little magic horse and a large retinue of

---

[6] [The original tale, "Das Zauberross," is to be found in Hedwig von Beit, *Symbolik des Märchens,* vol. 1, pp. 738ff.— Ed.]

24

slaves and animals. But along the way the Div begins eating first the slaves and then the animals, until they are all devoured.

The princess is full of terror, as they are approaching a cave. The little horse advises her to tell the Div to go on in and that they will follow him. As she and the pony enter the cave after the Div, she sees that it is full of skeletons. The pony tells her that the Div is going to eat her too, so she must beat him and get on him (the pony). This she does and they make their escape.

The Div is furious when he sees they have left, and he makes a snow storm so powerful that they cannot proceed. Then the magic horse tells her to throw the pink behind her. As she does this, all the plain between her and the Div is immediately transformed into heavy thorn bushes.

The Div calls to her, "Oh, dear little bride, you are so far away. What did you do to get through these thorn bushes?"

She answers, "I took off all my clothes until I was as naked as the day I was born, and then I came through."

The Div removes his clothing, and of course he has an even more devilish time. While he is working his way through, the princess and the little horse continue their flight.

But at last the Div does get through, and soon he is close behind them again. Now the magic horse tells the girl to throw the salt behind her. This is immediately transformed into a great sandy desert and a salty sea between the Div and the fleeing pair.

Again the Div calls to his bride far away, "Oh, dear one, how did you get through this sand and sea?"

She answers again, "I took off all my clothes until I was as naked as the day my mother bore me."

Again the Div removes his clothes, which makes his progress through this forbidding waste land even more difficult, and again this gives the princess and the magic horse time to get away.

But of course it is only a breathing spell, because the Div does eventually cover the distance between them and is nearly upon them for the third time when the magic horse tells her it is time to throw the comb behind her.

This time it is a giant mountain that rises between them and the pursuing Div. When the Div asks his bride how she got through it, she tells him she pulled out two teeth and tried to make a hole through the mountain. Following this procedure, the Div is naturally delayed a long time, and the horse and the girl get far ahead.

But as before, the Div finally gets through, and now he is very angry as for the fourth time they are almost within his reach. Prompted by the horse, the girl throws the mirror behind her, and the land transforms into a wide and roaring river.

The Div calls to her, "Oh, dear bride, what did you do to get across the river?"

She answers, "I put around my neck a big stone and plunged into the waters."

The Div does this and then disappears from the story for the time being.

The girl and the horse finally come to a hut in which live a little old man and woman, who invite them to stay. Next morning the girl falls asleep near the hut. The king of the area has meanwhile been out hunting and become lost. His servants find the king's hawk sitting on the princess's head. The king asks who she is. The girl had asked the old couple to say, if anyone asks, that she is their daughter, which they do. Although the king believes them, it doesn't make any difference to him that she is of such lowly birth, and he asks her to marry him. So they marry and are very happy.

One day the king decides to go out hunting again and to stay away for eight or nine months. The girl doesn't much like this, and is even more concerned when he wants to take her little horse with him. But the horse tells her not to be afraid; she must take some hair from his mane, and she should burn it when she is in danger, and he will be there.

In the meantime, the Div has escaped from the stream and is bent on vengeance. He assumes the form and clothes of a humble laborer and waits for his opportunity.

While the king is away the queen gives birth to twin sons, and a messenger is sent to the king with a letter telling him about the event. This is the chance the Div has been waiting for. He sends a terrific rain storm to hinder the messenger, and in the confusion the Div changes the letter so that the message reads that the queen has given birth to a dog and a cat.

When the king receives this message he is dismayed and sad, but sends back a letter saying not to harm the queen. This message too is intercepted by the Div, who arranges that the court receive an order to set the queen backward on an ass, together with the two sons, to blacken her face and send her out of the city in disgrace.

The Div comes upon her in this predicament, as she is sorrowfully leaving the city, and laughs at her. He says that he will now eat her, but will torture her first by eating the two children before her very eyes. The queen thinks quickly and says that at least he should make a proper feast out of them by building a fire to cook them. The Div builds the fire, which gives her an opportunity to burn the hair from the mane of the magic horse.

The magic horse promptly appears. He tells her that this is very serious, and that this time he will have to fight the Div. If blood or red foam appears in the stream, she will know that he has been killed by the Div; but if white foam appears, it will mean that all is well and the Div has been destroyed.

The fight takes place between the magic horse and the Div as the girl watches anxiously. Red foam appears, and the girl faints.

But when she wakes up she sees that the foam is white, and the horse is alive. He tells her that she is now safe from the Div forever, but he also tells her that now the time has come that must kill him, the horse. She must throw his head away, place his four legs in the four cardinal directions, throw the bowels away, and then sit with her children under the ribs.

The girl protests against killing the horse, but he convinces her that it must be done. She follows all his directions and finally sits with her children under his ribs. All the dismembered parts of the horse now transform themselves into a paradise: the legs turn into emerald trees; out of the bowels spring beautiful villages; the ribs turn into a golden castle; and out of the head comes a beautiful crystal river.

Meanwhile, the king has returned from hunting and discovered that his wife is gone. He is very angry as he realizes what has happened. In his fury and grief he kills all the people in the town and very nearly goes mad himself. After this holocaust he becomes a wandering dervish and sets out to look for his wife. Eventually he comes upon the beautiful paradise which had come into being by the sacrifice of the magic horse, and is delighted with the landscape and the golden castle.

A maid is drawing water at a well, and he asks her who lives in the golden castle. She tells him that it is the home of a widow and her two sons. He suspects that his search is at an end—that it is his wife who lives in this paradise—and while the maid is not looking he puts his ring into her water bucket.

The queen recognizes the ring and rushes out with her two sons to meet him. The family is reunited with rejoicing, and from then on they live together in this beautiful city.[7]

---

[7] [Additional commentary by Dr. von Franz on this story appears in *Shadow and Evil in Fairy Tales*, pp. 256ff.— Ed.]

*

Here the trap set by the king is not a glass mountain but a flea and its skin. Fleas and bugs in general belong to the devil—to the peasants he is the master of rats and bugs and fleas. The general feeling that these are devilish and demonic is due to their being parasites that suck our life blood—like an autonomous complex.

Flea is also a vulgar term for a whore. In the German language there is the expression "to make an elephant out of a louse," and in English, "to make a mountain out of a molehill." In *Faust,* Mephistopheles sings of the king who loved his flea, had him clothed by a tailor, and decreed that the lords and ladies must let him have his way with them without hindrance. He makes his heir and successor a flea, who bites the ladies. Making the heir so silly keeps him from being a serious threat to the ruling order.

In short, one makes a big thing out of a trifle in order to hold back life and prevent growth. This is a typical attitude of dying religions or political systems. When the flow of psychic energy is blocked, then come endless theological and philosophical quarrels; or, in academic life, silly dissertations over unimportant questions, while vital issues are ignored. That is a typical sign that true spiritual life has vanished, and therefore all the fleas come up.

Here again we have no queen, so the feeling life is lacking. When the feeling side of life is gone, then relationship degenerates into just sex as the only way to relate to another person. In cases where catatonics are being helped toward getting back into life, the first forms of relating come out in the most primitive expressions of sex. In the same way, wherever feeling life has degenerated, in all decaying civilizations, you see this very visible and tactless display of sexuality. In living civilizations it is more hidden, and is mixed with feeling.

This confirms the theory proposed in our discussion of "Old

Rinkrank," namely that the king is a reversion to the old Wotan in the German soul. We can say that the word "Div" is a degenerate form of "divine." In Abyssinia, the same figure is called "Zar"; possessed women are called "brides of Zar," and there are dance rituals for the curing of such women. They have the feeling that it is not good for a woman to be alone, for if she is alone she generally picks up some Zar as a kind of ghostly lover, and so men should stay away from her.

In the beginning of our story, the slave at the king's court betrays the secret of the flea's skin. The slave in fairy tales is a frequent carrier for projection of the naive, uncivilized, lowest level of awareness. The betrayal of a secret by a slave or someone lowly is a common motif—the murmuring of what is going on, which is then overheard by a ghost or witch. Sometimes the slave murmurs into a reed and the reed gives away the secret, or a shepherd cuts a reed for a pipe and the pipe betrays it.

If one's unconscious complex is activated, you cannot stop it. It creeps through the door. People who cannot possibly know about it may even dream about it. This is due to the penetrating force of unconscious complexes, the infectious quality of which needs more research and studying. Jung once told me of a man who had identified a certain style of dreaming among his family members, and then discovered that the dreams of friends who stayed in the house with them were full of similar motifs. There is such a thing as an "atmosphere of the house." This relates to the mythological motif that if there is an unconscious content of vital importance, something that should be known and not kept secret, it will somehow come out.

In this story it is not coming up from the unconscious into consciousness, but rather the reverse: a Div picks up this secret flow of energy to the unconscious which cannot be stopped. When the ruling attitude is no longer adequate, there is a loss of libido, which then sinks into the unconscious where it constellates a compensating figure. Here it constellates the beggarman, the Div, and the king is forced to gives his daughter away, as he promised. He wants to keep his position, but at the same time he wants to undermine his position.

The same motif appears in an old German tale where the king's daughter is haughty and rejects all who woo her. The king becomes angry and says, "Well, you'll have to accept the next beggar who comes along"—and then he has to keep his promise. Here the king tries not to keep his promise, but the Div shows his power and the king gives in.

The Div represents the darker, more archaic form or image of God. The daughter belongs to a particular civilization. The anima is usually one step behind, and therefore the animus is also represented by a very primitive, pagan God. The anima of ancient Greece was generally represented as a foreign slave, a foreign princess of a more primitive tribe. In medieval times, the anima became pagan, appearing as a Greek or Roman goddess. We might speculate that in time she may become Christian. Since this is a fairy tale of Islamic times, the animus would be a pre-Islamic, pagan demon.

The Div now produces a cap which, when he throws it up in the air, becomes or creates a black fog; then he throws it down and it creates light. He can use the cap to create storms, like a weather demon. We speak of someone being "under the weather." This shows the difference in style between the tactics used by the anima and the animus.

The animus produces emotional, stormy arguments, whereas the anima is subject to subtle moods that come out in spoiling remarks. The animus is prone to brutal demonstrations of his power—brute force. The anima has more cunning ways to get what she wants or to make her presence known.

A cap covers the head, and so in general is associated with one's *Weltanschauung,* one's world view or ultimate concepts. In fairy tales there are various kinds of caps. If it is a nebulous cap, like fog and so on, it produces confusion. In dreams we often see disorderly hair, which shows animus confusion. "Her head was just a nest of plots"—wanting to play all sorts of tricks at the same time. "She got into a snarl of confusion"—wanting to say "just the right thing," and so in the end could say nothing. The animus loves to create a misty atmosphere, an ambiance in which one cannot find one's orientation. The spreading of a cloud over a country is also attributed to dwarfs and giants— because they disturb consciousness.

The king is so frightened by the Div's demonstration that he hands his daughter over. She goes into a stable where there is a magic horse who later becomes the saving factor. It is interesting that this saving factor is in the stable of the king, the same place where the whole difficulty begins. We can take the horse here as a bisexual force, although in the end it turns into a beautiful city, which is a feminine image. The missing mother, the queen, is probably in this horse.

In fairy tales where the mother is dead or has disappeared— regressed into the animal layer of the psyche—she typically becomes the helpful instinct for the daughter.

Jung once suggested to me that the high, pointed caps of dwarfs mean that unconscious contents are trying to push up into consciousness. One might call it a phallic symbol, in the sense of an activity that wants to shoot up. If caps appear with such points, we don't need to do anything about the matter— there is enough energy in them that they will come up on their own. For instance, there is a kind of animus thinking about love which destroys a woman's real feeling. She thinks, "Shall I or shall I not go to bed with him?" rather than, "How do I feel about him?" or "Do I love him?"

The wrong conscious attitude calls forth a counter-reaction from the unconscious, and then there is a panic. After the Div's demonstration of power, the king must now give in. Here the king represents a conscious attitude which is completely helpless toward the unconscious. Had his attitude been adequate, he would have called in a magician of his own. Panic attacks are always a symptom of weak ego consciousness which cannot cope with the unconscious and fears being overwhelmed by it.

The helpful animal here is not a wild animal, but a domesticated horse in the stable. This would indicate that the split between the animal layer and the civilized layer is not too great.

You can read the cultural situation of a land from its fairy tales. This story comes from Turkestan. In the Christian Western world there is much more of a split, and thus much more tension. Orientals have developed their civilization so slowly and gradually that there is not the kind of split there that we find in Western civilization. They have a deeper wisdom—but because there is not much tension from splitting, the negative side is that there is less potential of energy. The one time they had a big *élan* was when Mohammed created monotheism to replace polytheism, but now again they have a low potential energy.

The symbolism of the horse generally falls into the bisexual category, as is the case with a tree. When we speak of "masculine" or "feminine" symbols, it is only a nuance in any case. In fact, the horse is one of the most difficult animals to interpret. The fox usually represents cunning, as well as some cruelty— cold, cold hate and grim rage—but the horse is just horse power. Horses are very sensitive to the ghost world, very much given to panic; they can take the bit in their mouth and run. But mainly the horse is *force,* and a helpful carrying force if we know how to treat it.

Then there is the beggar motif. The Div, then the girl, and then the king all go through the beggar stage. In the fairy tale "King Thrushbeard," where the haughty girl must marry the beggar—and so is completely humiliated—the beggar reveals that he is really a king who only appeared as Thrushbeard in order to provide her redemption through the necessary first step of humiliation. Here the king and the beggar are compensating sides of the same entity. And in our tale the Div comes out of the pool as compensation to the king's too-lofty attitude.

We have a tendency to think of "high" and "up" as meaning consciousness, with "down" or "under" referring to the unconscious, but looking at it from a natural viewpoint, that is obviously wrong. In the primitive point of view, the world or middle level represents consciousness, while both the heavens above and the underworld are different realms of unconsciousness. Certainly one who is "up in the clouds" is not conscious, but the subject is much too complicated to speak simply of "up" and "down."

The primitive picture generally refers to the form or pattern of the instincts, with the upper realm containing the archetypes as spiritual elements. Our conscious world is in the middle, and below it are the archetypes as physical instincts. The upper and lower worlds are both in the unconscious; they are two archetypes of the same thing.

Early Christianity arose in compensation for a decaying civilization where people were living a lower-than-animal life, in a perverted swamp; hence the dreams of the early Christians contained images of going with a ladder *up* to heaven, going up toward spirituality. This was a necessary compensatory process. Today, where we have gone too far "up" and away from the instincts, compensating dreams involve going "down."

We cannot even speak of mother goddesses as being always "below," as they were conceptualized in Greece. In Egypt the earth god was masculine; spiritual things were concrete, because the earth god was male.

When the Div comes up out of the pool, it means that the ruling principle has gone too far away from the instincts. Therefore it must be the horse that is the redeeming factor. They have all been too high, therefore they must all be humiliated—be beggars—before they can be redeemed. We have all experienced the new sense of power that comes when we have sunk down in the sea and finally our feet touch solid ground, leading to a spurt of energy that enables us to rise again. So here they must all go down and become "Div-ified," acquiring what he had, and then they can come up again. Here the Div is specifically only negative, devouring human life and leaving nothing but the bones

The motif of running away, escaping, is also familiar from other tales, where running away from the demon is the only successful solution. In many instances, to escape the unconscious in a certain aspect is just as heroic a deed as conquering the dragon. It is quite difficult enough just to run away, escaping back into the human realm.

Throwing things backward without looking is the pagan gesture of sacrificing to the unnamable, the untouchable chthonic god, the gesture of worship to the dark powers which you cannot look at, cannot face. This is important to know psychologically, because we are so caught up in the Christian attitude of having to "face" everything. There are dark things which have numinous qualities which we cannot face; we can only sacrifice to them, which is to recognize their power.

In psychotics, for instance, there are things so dark that it would not be wise to pull them up and look at them; one can only sacrifice to them but not look back at them. So the princess cannot face this terrible Div, but she sacrifices to him without looking at him. She sacrifices three items which reflect her feminine persona: the flower, the comb and the mirror, as well as salt, which we will discuss later. It is said that roses have thorns because there is no love without thorns—that is, negative remarks and feelings.

The shadow is a positive function; it has a vital instinct which can help. We could say that the shadow is positive as long as it stays in the inner world and does not act up in the outer world, where it is the province of the persona to move and act and protect one. The Div comes up against the girl's own negative feminine side, which stops him for awhile; it gives him "a lot to chew on."

What does that mean in practice, to give the shadow something to chew on? Animus possession may take the form of criticizing everybody and everything—and the damnable thing about the animus is that he is quite right, but likely to be wrong in the specific situation. A way to stop the arguing and criticizing is for the woman to say to her animus, "If you are so terribly fanatical about what is wrong and what 'should' be, let's look at my shadow." Then there is an impact inside which is very helpful to the woman in sorting out what *she* really believes.

Women don't have such a desire as men have to be perfect. But if there is a strong animus, then there is a correspondingly strong shadow, and by confronting one with the other women have a chance to become conscious. In other words, if a woman has a strong animus, and can overcome her reluctance to knowing her shadow, she can develop a degree of male objectivity about what goes on in her and thereby become conscious. She must learn to tell the difference between herself and her opinions, between her feminine ego and her masculine animus. And if she cannot, she will suffer endless relationship problems.

There is always a step in the individuation of a woman where she must give up the magic power she possesses over men on account of the projection of their anima. She must sacrifice her identification with such projections if she wants to acquire an individual personality. Jung once said that where love is lacking, power jumps in. A woman with a strong animus has a prestige persona which she tries to protect. That is power.[8]

Salt has a double aspect. In alchemy, salt is the symbol of wisdom, but it also has a stinging quality of bitterness—the bitterness of the sea comes from the salt in it. Wisdom, wit, bitterness and Eros—all that is associated with salt.[9] Jung says this has to do with a specific feminine feeling of love: when a woman is disappointed in love, she becomes either bitter or wise, developing a sense of humor or a certain wit.[10] Eros is always combined with disappointment—anyone who really loves must risk disappointment; the wisdom of love comes in accepting the disappointment without bitterness.

The comb has to do with putting one's hair in order—it is an object symbolically associated with organizing one's thoughts. In our story the comb transforms itself into a mountain, which is a good way to express what a woman must present to the animus to chew its way through.

---

[8] ["Where love reigns, there is no will to power; and where the will to power is paramount, love is lacking. The one is but the shadow of the other." ("On the Psychology of the Unconscious," *Two Essays on Analytical Psychology,* CW 7, par. 78)—Ed.]

[9] [See "The Personification of the Opposites," *Mysterium Coniunctionis,* CW 14, par. 330.—Ed.]

[10] ["Disappointment, always a shock to the feelings, is not only the mother of bitterness but the strongest incentive to a differentiation of feeling. The failure of a pet plan, the disappointing behavior of someone one loves, can supply the impulse either for a more or less brutal outburst of affect or for a modification and adjustment of feeling, and hence for its higher development. This culminates in wisdom if feeling is supplemented by reflection and rational insight. Wisdom is never violent: where wisdom reigns there is no conflict between thinking and feeling." (Ibid., par. 334)—Ed.]

The mirror is an instrument of reflection. It literally reflects back to us what we can see of ourselves on the outside—how we appear to others. At the same time, when we reflect on ourselves, on our reactions to others and their reactions to us, we have the chance to know ourselves better. When a woman comes to grips with her animus, when she reflects on his influence in her life, he drowns in her reflections, while she herself is saved from drowning.

The question that arises in this story is, did the girl sacrifice these things—the flower, the comb, the mirror and the salt—or merely throw them away? There is a difference between throwing away and sacrificing. Sacrificing, in pagan times, had a ritual meaning. The horse tells the girl to take these things with her, and later tells her when to throw them back. So who is in charge, the girl (her ego) or the horse (representing her instinct)? And does it matter which?

Only by sacrificing what we have can we know what we have. Real sacrifice is made with the same definiteness and lack of bargaining that is involved in throwing something away. We can do this only if we are forced to by a greater power in us—a power stronger than the ego—that gives us the necessary strength. We experience this power as an inner imperative which tells us that we "must." In Jungian psychology we understand that as a message from the Self, the regulating center of the psyche. The sacrificer and what is sacrificed are one and the same: it is always the Self. When the girl sacrifices what is precious to her, she has a chance to realize the true meaning of her life.

You may recall what I said about walking away from a conflict. This can be misunderstood. It is not meant as a cheap escape in order to avoid the conflict. The girl here is running for her life. Naturally, one has to have a conflict before it is a question of walking out of it. There are people who avoid conflict altogether by shutting themselves up in a rational system and refusing to face their own darkness. Here we must assume that the girl is already in a terrific conflict, but she has at hand the means to deal with it, thanks to her instinct, personified in the magic horse and the tools he tells her to take on their journey.

In day-to-day life, one has the chance to step aside until one recovers. This is in the end not a definitive solution, for eventually one must face the conflict. Women can be tortured by the animus, who tells them they are a complete failure, that their life is finished and now it is too late. The thing to do then is to say, "Okay, I am a failure; let's not discuss it any more." This is a sort of stepping out of it, and thus one saves energy and can turn to something else. This is like throwing a part of ourselves to the animus—let him eat it and in this way stop him from hindering our further action.

In our tale, we have the motif of recovering. The girl arrives at a hut and finds the poor old man and woman who allow her to stay the night. She is so exhausted she falls asleep outside the hut. In the morning the king's hawk alights on her head and thus the king finds her. That is how she comes to marry him.

In the old beggar couple she has for the first time a positive father and mother—the wisdom of the spirit and the wisdom of the earth, so to speak. Think of the Greek story of Philemon and Baucis, who entertained Zeus and Hermes in disguise, and who, because of their piety, were spared by the gods when everyone else was destroyed in the flood. In Goethe's *Faust,* Faust kills this old couple due to his inflation.[11]

Every possession by the animus is a secret inflation, like every possession by the anima in a man. The anima and animus are suprapersonal to a great extent; they belong to the divine

---

11 [See Edward F. Edinger, *Goethe's Faust: Notes for a Jungian Commentary,* pp. 81ff.—Ed.]

realm, the collective unconscious, whereas the shadow belongs to the personal unconscious. If you check on the standards used by the animus in his constant criticism, you find that they are always a collective truth, something much beyond the individual. Therefore every identification with it is a secret inflation, which is different from the visible inflation that can be so annoying.

That is why the humble couple provides a sort of cure—with them she recovers. This is one more form of escaping animus possession: taking on a humble attitude. When you go around saying, "You should do such and such," it means, "I am the person who is in a position to tell people what they should do." That is god-like; it is an inflation of the ego. The way to get out of such a state of possession is to be humble, to admit that you might be a failure, that you might not know, and so on.

As soon as the girl is low enough—a beggar's child, in effect—she falls into a state of unconsciousness, and thereby new life comes to her. When people put themselves high up, it is like standing on a mountain: all the water of life flows away from them. But down in the valley the water can reach them.

It is the king's hawk that sits on her head. In the Orient, the hawk is a divine bird, a royal bird. So we can say the girl is chosen by the spirit to be the king's bride. This king too is an animus figure, if we take the tale from the feminine viewpoint, but he would represent a spiritual attitude which is more than just a contrast to the feminine.

We are inclined to think of spirit and nature, Logos and Eros, etc., as total opposites, but this is not really so. A genuine spiritual attitude which lacks the negative quality of the animus does not oppose real feminine life. It is what gives objective understanding; it is a creative force, providing inspiration for the men in a woman's life. This is the nature of the positive animus, which makes it possible for her to have objective and creative attitudes toward life. If a woman is "only" a woman, this implies a certain degree of inertia, but the positive animus enables her to be active and creatively enterprising. This is a positive aspect of the king on the personal level.

With this new king there is a new dominant collective attitude. This corresponds to the fact that when a woman overcomes her animus problems, then she will belong to the new spirit of her time, taking part in it and even bringing it about. In the rise of Christianity, for instance, the earliest converts were mostly women.

Women in general have this tendency—to take up new ideas, new movements, because their mind (the animus in them) is less bound by tradition. In a way, no theory about life is quite as important to women as it is to men. In the negative sense, it means also that women are not completely committed to what they say they believe. This is because love and relationships mean more to them than do theoretical questions. But, on the other hand, they can pick up a new idea more easily than can a man who is committed to a particular *Weltanschauung*.

I once knew a professor of physics who was frightened when he listened to some of the new speculations. He said that if he thought they were true he would go out and hang himself because "all is lost if I must now acknowledge that everything I have been teaching is wrong." This attitude is natural for men, who are much more committed to their concepts than are women. Men really feel like an earthquake has hit if their view of life is called into question.

Women are not committed to specific ideas (though their animus may be), and that is why they are able to contribute to the renewal of collective attitudes. Also, in general, if a woman has a positive father complex, she is somehow better able to come to terms with the spiritual problems of her time—she cannot live just the physical side of her life. And that is why the woman who leaves the traditional path of the superficial form of feminine life becomes a queen.

And so in our tale the girl marries the king—but then the story starts all over again! This is typical of Oriental fairy tales, which usually end with a link—done in just the right way—that starts a new story. Here the queen becomes pregnant and the king goes away to hunt, asking to take the magic horse with him, since he can't see that she will have any use for it while she is pregnant. At first she is afraid, but the horse reassures her, giving her some hairs of his mane which she can burn if necessary.

Why must the king go away? We don't really know, but we can assume that the solution of the first part of the tale—their happy marriage—is not in accord with real life; that is, there are still certain aspects of their life that have not been integrated. This happens to people in analysis: they feel "finished" for a time, and then later discover parts that still need integrating, or feel the need to amplify their consciousness. Here we cannot explain why the king goes off, but clearly he is possessed by a passion for hunting. Perhaps too he is not satisfied with his home, or is bored with his pregnant wife. There has been a certain solution, you see, but there is still some restlessness. The animus does this to compensate for natural feminine inertia.

The king taking the horse means that he goes away with the vital, carrying powers. Certain individuals have the need to enlarge their personality. Such a person is more liable to experience difficulties in life than is a weaker person. Something in them wants to get into trouble, so to speak, because of the need to use their energy in the pursuit of self-realization. So, the life force is on the side of restlessness, which comes out in hunting for a new adventure.

Meanwhile, the queen is brooding something in her pregnant

state. When people are restless, like a prancing horse in a stable, we can be pretty sure that the psyche is pregnant. But, on the other hand, if the animus breaks loose ahead of time, if it hasn't the patience to wait, then the negative side of the animus comes in. If the king had stayed home, not been impatient, then he could probably have met and fought the Div, disposed of him.

The animus is frequently like this, too impatient: a woman feels she must make up her mind immediately, cut through a situation, act one way or another, instead of waiting for the pregnant psyche to bring forth the proper new development.

So, the Div seizes his chance for revenge, and intercepts the letters regarding the birth of the children and the treatment of the queen. Here the negative animus appears in a new form—that of falsifying the messages which come from the unconscious to consciousness, and from consciousness to the unconscious.

In practice, a woman can understand with her heart what is really meant by something said to her, but later in the evening, say, she begins to get suspicious of just how it was said, why it was said in that way, etc., etc. The animus has intercepted the message and put his own poison into it.

The Div changes the first letter to read that the queen has given birth to a cat and a dog. He falsifies the second letter to arrange that she will be humiliated and sent out of the city in disgrace. This is the work of the negative animus, who destroys what should be born from the inside, disparaging it as "nothing but" this or that. He completely humiliates a woman, turning her against herself and against the future life she carries within.

In medieval times it was a common custom to put women who were accused as whores on an ass, seated backward, and then to drive them out of town. Here the animus is trying to make the girl think like that about herself.

When they are out in the desert the Div shows his hand, saying to the queen, "Now I am going to eat you." But she is clever enough to trick him, giving him some cooking advice. She says he might as well have a good meal by building a fire and brewing up a stew out of the boys he is going to eat first. In practical life this sometimes works—appearing to accept what the animus says. For example, he may tell her, "My man doesn't love me any more." One pretends to accept that, and says, "Well, perhaps I don't deserve to be loved," and then one can find peace. Through this appeasement of the animus, one may find one's true feelings and discover that it was all animus talk.

The burning of the horse's hair and the immediate appearance of the horse bring up the idea of the relativity of space and time in the unconscious: what seems far away can actually be present if one sees the connection. It is what happens in the case of mental telepathy.

The horse appears and explains that the time has come for him to fight the Div. He says she will not see the fight but will know if red foam appears that he has been killed by the Div, and that if white foam appears it means the horse has killed the Div. The fight takes place. The girl thinks she sees red foam and faints dead away. When she wakens, she sees that it is white foam, and the horse is there to tell her that her troubles with the Div are now permanently over. Then the horse says it is time for her to kill him, and tells her how she must dispose of his various parts. At first she resists, but finally does as she is told.

We see here that she herself is not engaged in the battle. The real fight goes on between two superpersonal powers. This is a common motif in fairy tales. There is one northern tale which tells of a woman who was expelled from her home. First she marries the moon god, but commits some sins so he sends her away. Then she marries the Kali, an evil, spirit-eating man. When she realizes he has eaten her brother, she escapes with the help of a fox. She goes toward heaven, till she reaches the polar star, which represents the supreme and good god in this land where the real polar star is so necessary to the people.

The evil Kali follows her and demands his wife back. The polar star puts him in a box and stirs up a wild snow storm, then opens the box and asks Kali, "Do you still want her?" The Kali says yes, so the process is repeated, again and again in ever increasing severity, until the Kali finally says, "No." When the Kali is disposed of, the polar star says she may now go back down to earth—but she fails to sacrifice to the polar star and so she dies, unable to go back to heaven.

Every animus conflict, if it is serious enough, seems to touch these deepest, archetypal layers of the psyche where there is an ongoing conflict between the light god and the dark god. That is why we should try to stand outside the conflict and at the same time watch it, try to realize it objectively. If a woman tries to step into the conflict between good and evil, she can only become caught in the animus. Her responsibility is just to take part in life itself, to guarantee the continuity of life outside.

In Persia, only the men are required to pledge themselves to fight against the dark god. The women must only keep life going and preserve human relatedness. It seems as though to suffer fate is the right attitude for a woman, not to try to take action in it. Here in our story, in the decisive event, the girl faints and doesn't even witness it.

Previously, the time had not yet come when the horse felt it was the right moment to fight. This seems to have to do with the fact that the queen now has children—the future has been born. The old quaternity looked like this:

```
First King--------------------------Princess
      |                                 |
Horse---------------------------------Div
```

In the end we have this situation:

```
Second King------------------------Queen
     |                              |
   Boy--------------------------------Boy
```

This is a new form of the *Auseinandersetzung*, the confrontation of opposites. The horse and the Div cancel each other out in the end. The horse is the power of life; the Div is a power of death. The horse could not risk the fight until there was a new possibility, represented by the two boys, of carrying the life force. It is only the animal form of the horse which is linked with the Div, and when the Div is killed then the horse is transformed into its true nature, the beautiful garden.

There is this same situation in a Siberian tale where a big mouth chases a girl until she comes upon three princes who have been waiting for her, and who give her her choice of which one to marry. Here the Div has the positive function of goading her on until she comes to the place where she meets herself. Women go through the process of individuation mainly by suffering, when it is done in the right way; in the unconscious there then seems to be a shifting of the libido. If one can adapt to the devil without being eaten by him, that makes for consciousness.

The horse tells her that after she has killed him, she is to put one of his legs in each of the four cardinal points, throw his head away on one side, throw his bowels away, and then sit with her children under his ribs.

This mirrors another common motif in fairy tales: the killing of the helpful animal after a given time. One such tale tells of the helpful fox who finally asks that his head and paws be cut off, and when this is done he turns into a prince who had been bewitched into fox form. Generally, the one restored to human form explains afterward that he had once been a human being and his animal form was due to a curse, and that he had wanted that form of himself to be killed.

If a woman dreams of her feminine nature as an animal, say a cat or a cow, she cannot integrate this but can only relate to it. But if it appears in human form, it has reached a level where it can be integrated. If it appears as a god, again we cannot integrate it, but can only relate to it.

A content of the psyche which has had a human shape but by a curse has been changed into an animal form, means a regression has occurred. The erotic life in late antiquity was relatively differentiated. But this period came to an end and further development was cut off by the arrival of Christianity. This meant an enormous advance in consciousness, on a much higher level. But in the field of the anima, of Eros, it was cut off completely. In antiquity there was a much higher level of relationship to the anima than in the Middle Ages.

There is an Irish tale about mermaids: A chief heard of the approach of the Christians, and swore that "those damn Christians" would not get hold of his daughters. So he threw a net over them and turned them into mermaids—who now splash around trying to lure men. These mermaids had been human, but through a wrong conscious attitude have been kept in an instinctive form. Eros in the Middle Ages, for example, regressed into pure sex without feeling—just the animal act. The spiritual implication of sexual relations wasn't seen; that regressed into the unconscious in the form of mermaids, fantasies, witches, etc.

If an animal asks to be redeemed, it is an act of discernment, a realization that in the physical instinct there is a spiritual side which could be humanized. With this discernment, one has to attack something which has previously been a help, as in the overcoming of self-pity or self-indulgence, in a field where one has been going along fine before. People with a sound inner instinct can sail smoothly through life for years and years, as simple peasants do, for instance; their horse carries them through. To a certain extent this is an enormous advantage; but it can become a disadvantage in that if people are too sound and down to earth, they remain quite unconscious because they have never differentiated themselves enough from the animal to become conscious of what it is. That is why the human instinct itself sometimes asks for the neurosis—asks for the deviation, for the split, in order to become conscious.

The instinctive drive is not one-sided but contains its own counter-drive, its own sacrificial drive. It contains its own sublimation, its own counteraction, which in the end comes forth and makes itself felt. The battle between the horse and the Div mirrors the natural split of the libido. Psychic libido is an antimony, its own contradiction.

Since this story is from Turkestan, which shared some symbolism with India, it is important to understand the Indian attitude toward the horse.[12] According to the Upanishads, the horse represents the whole world, and is a sacrificial horse. To paraphrase, the dawn is the head, the sun is the eye, the wind his breathing, universal fire his open mouth. The hair of the horse is the Atman, the sky his back. The atmosphere is his belly, water his flanks, the seasons his limbs, day and night his feet. His voice is creative speech. The horse's place is the eastern sea. The night is the sacrificial vessel which remains behind; its place is the western sea. Note that in our tale, the battle takes place in the water.

As an illustration of the secret relationship between the Div, or spirit of death, and the horse, the Upanishads continue:

In the beginning was nothing; all was covered with death—

---

[12] [The source for the following remarks on the symbolism of the horse in the Upanishads is not known.—Ed.]

with hunger, for hunger is death. In time water was produced. The water was brightness. Out of the water the earth was formed, then came fire and wind. The world as horse is creative power, which is a symbol for the libido. Those who sacrifice the horse transcend the world and live in the wind, which is a little space between heaven and the world, no bigger than a razor blade. (There's the idea of the smallness of the Self.)

Looking at our fairy tale from this Indian angle, we see now what the horse sacrifice means: the animal, instinctive libido turns into its own opposite—that is what leads to individuation, which is a natural process of growth. All we have to do is not to disturb it, simply to accompany it with understanding and with endurance. Individuation is given to our nature; to be oneself is the most natural process in the world.

That is why in the end the horse turns into a natural paradise. But what is not complete is that the garden is a symbol of the mother, a symbol of the womb. The horse turns into a containing vessel. The killing of the horse is the Indian solution, which leaves the animal, and leaves the world, transcending the instinct. But it is not complete, because it is outside reality.

The other aspect of incompleteness is that the queen gives birth to twin boys. At this point we have four human beings—an advance over the first quaternity, which included the horse and the Div—but there is an overbalance on the male side, with the sons being germs of the future. Since the earth belongs to the feminine, if it is missing it means a spiritual solution only. This is the Indian solution, though not a satisfactory one for most of us in the West.

The Greeks also knew the twins motif. The twins represent a double impetus of the libido, a new movement toward the development of consciousness, which is still a germ, incomplete, and still outside the bounds of reality. In Jungian psychology we know it as the "doubling motif," which manifests when an unconscious content is on the brink of becoming conscious, at which point the opposites—which in the unconscious are one—fall apart into two.[13]

According to our tale, the twins are brothers and not animals (cat and dog, as in the Div's false message). But I have never found a fairy tale yet that is complete in the end. That is not surprising; they could not show completeness because there is no individual in them. Only individuals can experience completeness, individuation.

A fairy tale is a *pattern*. A pattern can only be a sketch, can only illustrate or bring to light certain laws of functioning; it cannot represent the complete goal, because for the realization of completeness the individual as the carrier of the process is needed. And that is the feminine aspect, the earth, which here is lacking. The solution in life is always individual. We cannot read a fairy tale and have the complete solution; the tale shows only how the libido is flowing in the collective human psyche.

There is, then, no completion here to the animus problem, though it ends with two boys, representing a higher level than in the beginning. The feminine Self must be present for completeness. Here the Self is represented as the horse, and then as the city which is a paradise, that is, only the light side. Missing is the dark aspect of the feminine, such as a witch, and with that being left out there is excluded also the material reality of the woman, the physical earth.

---

[13] [For more extensive comments on the doubling motif, see von Franz, *On Divination and Synchronicity: The Psychology of Meaningful Chance*, pp. 105-109; also Edward F. Edinger, *The Aion Lectures: Exploring the Self in C.G. Jung's* Aion, pp. 101f.—Ed.]

3
Kari, the Girl with the Wooden Frock

In this Norwegian tale, there was a widower king who had a beautiful daughter. He married a second time, and the stepmother was very jealous of the girl, abusing her relentlessly.

Among the king's cattle there was a big blue bull who was very clean, and so the daughter would run away from the palace and spend most of her time with him. In his ear the bull carried a magic tablecloth, which the princess would spread out and then it would provide her with food.

When the stepmother discovered this, she was very angry and hysterical. She went to bed and pretended that her illness could only be cured by eating the flesh of the bull. The girl and the bull learned of her intention to have him killed, and made their escape together.

By and by they came to a forest made completely of brass. The bull said to the girl, "Don't touch any of the brass leaves, for if you do I will have to fight the troll with three heads who lives in the forest. But if you can't avoid touching the leaves, and the troll does come out and fight, then take the ointment which is in my other ear and use it to heal me."

The girl couldn't help touching the leaves, and the three-headed troll came out and fought with the bull. The bull won, but was exhausted and injured; however the girl cured him with the magic ointment and they continued on their way.

The second forest they came to was all of silver, and the situation was the same except that the troll was six-headed. The third forest was all of gold, and the troll there had nine heads. In each case the girl could not avoid touching the leaves, so the fight with the troll had to take place, followed by the magic curing of the bull with the ointment.

Finally they arrive at a castle, and here the bull says, "This is the end of my help. You must sleep in a pigsty and wear a wooden frock. But first you must kill me, skin me, and then put into the skin one brass leaf, one silver leaf and one gold apple. Roll up the skin and put it under this rock, and if you are ever in difficulty knock on the rock and you will get help."

The girl does as she is bidden, and then begins a period of servitude as a lowly maid in the castle. She is given a wooden frock to wear and told to carry the bath water up to the prince. She clumps and bumps along in her stiff wooden frock, and the prince is infuriated by the noise and her clumsiness. He kicks her out, throwing his towel after her.

Upset and distressed, she goes and knocks on the rock. Immediately there appears the spirit of a man who gives her a frock made of brass, which she wears to church. The prince goes to church and sees her in the beautiful brass frock and on a brass horse, and his mind is not at all on the church service. After church he tries to catch up with her, but she repeats a charm:

> Light before me
> Darkness behind me.
> So that the prince shan't see where I am going.

The prince loses sight of her then, though he does catch one of her gloves. When he asks her later where she came from, she replies, "Towel Land."

The same drama is repeated twice more, the next time involving a silver gown, the charm as before, and the prince catching her comb, with her again naming the land she came from after the towel he had throw at her. The third time it is a golden dress she wears, and a golden shoe she loses to the prince. Always she uses the same magic charm to prevent him from catching up with her.

As in the story of Cinderella, the prince then sends out all over the land to find the lady whose foot fits the golden shoe. The stepmother tries to trick him by cutting off part of her foot, but the blood is discovered in the shoe. Finally the rightful owner, Kari, is found in the kitchen in a wooden frock. She reveals her royal background and she marries the prince.

*

Having a stepmother means that one is cut off from the feeling function, which is replaced by something else. Stepmothers are always characterized as a "Frau Welt" (Mrs. World), a feminine personification of the outer world in its aspect of falseness, jealousy, vanity. Wherever Eros vanishes or fails, then up comes this prestige psychology. Wherever there is a real power drive, Eros is crippled. And also, when a ruling system stiffens because there is a lack of Eros, then you are sure to find a dominant power attitude—because the ruling system feels the earth slipping from beneath its feet.

Here the helpful animal is a bull, which can represent primitive masculinity, brutal emotion, often linked with the negative animus, who can really cause a woman to be like a bull in a china shop. But describing this bull as "blue" and "clean" means that here he is not destructive. Blue refers either to the sea or to the heavens. He is also a magic bull, with food in one ear and healing ointment in the other.

Sometimes the Self and the anima are one and the same thing, compacted into one personification. Here it is the feminine Self and the animus. And here again the fight is carried on not by the girl, but by the bull and the trolls.

The numbers three, six and nine are considered male, representing force, with the flow of energy increasing more and more according to the number of heads on the trolls. There is also an increase in the value of the metals: brass, silver and finally gold.

The fight between the bull and the trolls is always brought about by the fact that the girl touches a leaf. If she could have avoided touching the metal leaves, fighting the trolls would not have been necessary. Tree leaves generally represent a human individual as a mortal creature. In Homer's *Odyssey,* the human beings are represented as the many leaves of a tree—the family or clan which goes on living although the individual leaves (people) fall in the autumn. Leaves are the individual in the aspect of something transient and mortal. If the girl could keep away from individual human reality, there would be no conflict.

There are women who are so afraid of this battle that they stay out of this world—they seem to have no animus and no conflicts. They are like princesses going through the forest untouched. But they only remain untouched because they don't touch the reality of the mortal individual, the drama of human relationship. If they do touch it, this princess life stops, and the trolls and bulls break loose.

Here the girl cannot avoid touching the leaves of mortal reality in herself. So she finds herself in conflict between greed and the death force against the positive power; chaos versus order.

There is always a fourfold pattern in these tales. Here we find three of the same general thing: the forests of brass, silver and gold, and then a breathing space until the fourth appears—the castle. Then there are the brass, silver and golden frocks, with the fourth element being the prince. There are always three similar, parallel things, and then one different one, the fourth, which is now inclusive of the whole thing.

Brass is transient, ambiguous, decaying easily. It is associated with Venus, Eros. Silver is associated with the moon. It is easily blackened; it is weak and eventually wastes. Gold is the sun; it is incorruptible, resists everything, withstands every destructive, undermining influence.

Regarding the wooden frock, it is as if, just when the occasion demands that she be articulate, all she can do is clomp along stiffly and noisily!

Then comes the most interesting motif in this story: she always runs away from the prince when he tries to find her. It is only after the stepmother's duplicity is discovered and she is cut out of the story by being made to look ridiculous and so loses her power—only after this can the girl marry the prince and reveal her true identity. This initial secrecy may be because of the danger posed by the stepmother. In the charm the girl recites, she asks for "light before me," so that she can see where she is going, but he who follows her cannot see. If she did turn back to the prince, the stepmother would get her.

This shows the feminine relationship to the animus: by facing too directly what is desired or wanted, the power drive is constellated, represented by the stepmother. In order to keep one's feminine integrity, one must not look toward what one wants, but look only inside oneself and try to find the light. The danger comes when one touches reality, because the witch—who represents the world of power and prestige—will then come in and destroy everything.

For a woman, it often seems like a long incubation, encouraging the process until it can come out from inside.

4
The Magician of the Plain

This Bantu fairy tale is another animus story which will lead into the problem of the anima. It illustrates the numinous and uncanny background of animus figures.

In a Bantu family there is a son who doesn't want to marry any of the girls in the village, as his parents wish. Instead, he wants to go to a foreign country to look for a wife. His parents warn him, but he won't listen. While traveling through foreign places he falls in love with a girl and decides to marry her.

The parents of the girl advise her to take along a large group of female slaves and other helpers as a sort of wedding present, but she doesn't want to take anything except the bull of the tribe, the "Magician of the Plain." This is a buffalo bull, which possesses a thousand magic arts. Her tribe is upset about this and they try to prevent her, but she insists and finally manages to take the bull. She also carries some magic roots, herbs and medicines. Her husband is never able to see the bull, because it is always hidden behind her.

Back among the husband's tribe the couple establish their home. The bull magically does all the wife's work, plowing, planting and cooking, and she is very much admired by the villagers because everything is done so wonderfully. But one day the bull comes to her and says he can't go on working like this because he is so very hungry—he must have something to eat. However, the girl can't feed him without her husband knowing, and so she tells the bull just to go out and steal peas from the fields of the village. The villagers become angry and thoroughly aroused when they realize that someone is stealing their peas.

One day the husband is able to see the bull who was previously invisible to him. He shoots the bull and kills him. When the girl sees what has happened, she cuts off the bull's head and hides it and the bull's skin in the garden. Then in the night she secretly takes them out of hiding, puts them in a pot together with some magic elements, and sings this song:

Oh my father, Magician of the Plain,
Indeed they told me thou shalt go into deep darkness,
in all darkness.
Thou art a young sprout of the miraculous tree
which grew out of the winds,
devoured before the right time has come,
devoured by the worm.

The skin starts to come back to life, and the head moves. But just at that moment the husband discovers what she is doing and kills the bull again. The next night the girl goes out and tries again to bring the bull back to life, using the same magic elements and singing as before, but again the husband intervenes and the bull falls back dead. The third night the girl tries, but there is no more power left in the magic and it doesn't work.

So now the girl picks up the remnants of the skin and the head and puts them in a basket which she carries on her head, and without saying anything to anyone, she returns to her own tribe. Here she tells her people that the bull is dead. They are in a panic of despair at hearing this news; there is no longer any meaning in life for them. They sing the same song the girl had sung but it doesn't work, so they all kill themselves, even the children, until no one is left.

Meanwhile the husband had been searching for his wife. Having followed her to her tribe, he now finds them all dead, including his wife. Heartbroken, he returns to his parents who tell him he should have listened and obeyed them and taken a wife from his own village. They say it serves him right, and now he has lost all his money.

*

The animus figure appears here as a totem animal, the life principle of the girl's tribe, the guarantee of their prosperity. The bull gives meaning to life, and therefore when he is dead they have no *raison d'être*.

This story also shows why in primitive life there are such stringent marriage taboos, which prevent one from marrying the projections of one's own anima or animus. Individual choice is made impossible for that reason. This precaution is necessary because their ego consciousness is not strong enough yet to deal with the whole problem of the anima and animus. All the stories dealing with the anima or animus end tragically: either the woman disappears, the mermaid returns to the sea, etc., or there follows a complete catastrophe.

It is important to understand this, because we can see it in people today who blindly marry an anima or animus projection, which then leads to a situation where the couple is not able to deal with the problem.

Here the girl calls the buffalo bull "father," which shows that the animus is derived from the experience of her personal father. But there is an incompatibility between the god of her tribe and the tribal beliefs of her husband's people.

In "The Psychology of the Transference," Jung speaks of one of the most primitive means of dealing with the anima/animus problem, the so-called cross-cousin marriage.[14] There are a great many instances of marriage laws following this pattern. For instance there may be two divisions within a tribe—the Night people and the Day people, or the Grass people and the Water peo-

---

14 *[The Practice of Psychotherapy,* CW 16, pars. 422ff.—Ed.]

ple, etc.. A man cannot marry a woman within his own totem group. For example, if he is a Grass man, he must marry a Water woman. But when he does this, then the brother of the Water woman must marry the sister of the Grass man (the groom of the Water woman):

Grass man's sister	Water woman
Grass man	Water woman's brother

This mirrors the fact that primitive peoples do not experience any separateness of identity between inner factors and outer reality.

There has always been this endogamous tendency, to marry within a particular group. Incest was rife between gods and goddesses in the Greek pantheon, comparable in our story to the sister of the groom marrying the brother of the bride. But the exogamous tendency, to marry outside the tribe, overcomes the former, making a break between the divine realm and the human realm, and reinforcing it by taboos.

Very often among primitives the god and goddess were first a human man and his sister who committed incest. Many primitive stories have this theme. Then the two leave the tribe and go over the river and become figures of the "beyond"—gods and goddesses. From then on, you have the supernatural realm where the endogamous tendency is lived, and the human realm where the exogamous tendency is lived. There are severe laws against endogamy in the human realm because of the danger of being overwhelmed by the unconscious.

Our story concerns the god (the buffalo bull) who is drawn into the human realm. When this happens, catastrophe is bound to occur. One must respect the tribal god as something belonging to the divine realm, and not try to take it into everyday life.

Historically, we have first the primitive practice, where the endogamous tendency—incest—is lived only in the divine realm, between gods and goddesses, figures of the unconscious. Then in Egypt the god and goddess appear in human form: the Pharaoh and his sister are the only human beings who may commit incest. The next step appeared in alchemy, which probably derived its symbols from the Egyptian ritual. But in alchemy, where the quaternity was expressed as

King------------------------Queen
     | |
     | |
Man-------------------------Woman

the king and queen are also chemical substances, so at this stage it appears nearer the human being, because now it becomes part of the elements of our body. The next step is Jungian psychology, with the concepts of anima and animus.

In all the above quaternal relations there are the possibilities of relatedness of various kinds. For instance, a man may relate to his anima but not to another woman, or to a woman but not to his anima, and so on. Sometimes the relationship involves only the anima and the animus and not the human beings at all: anima and animus are attracted to one other, but when the two people are thrown together they may not be able to stand each other at all! In past times, these factors, anima and animus, were projected into the realm of kings and queens.

In our tale, the animus figure in the form of a bull cannot be made to live again when the husband sees the ritual; the very fact of the husband seeing it is what kills it. This is just what happens in everyday life. When a woman makes an attempt to develop her animus, the husband makes a natural attempt to shoot down the effects; and the wife likewise tries to destroy the development of the anima in her husband.

There is a legitimate secrecy during this process, which is necessary because of the incompatibility of these elements. For example, you often see a woman make a beginning toward developing her thinking function. She starts in a typically feminine way, perhaps with a quite second-rate book, but becomes absorbed in it, really excited. The husband notices that and says, "Well, if you are going to take that up, you should begin this or that way, read this or that," and so on; his Logos wants to organize her interest systematically, and by doing that he kills it.

Similarly, when the husband is trying to develop his feeling function, he may begin by doing very silly things, sloppy and sentimental, and the natural Eros of the woman resents it, causing her to intervene with, say, a condescending remark, which kills the whole development.

The path of these archetypes meanders like a stream in a swamp. The partner in whom a particular function is better developed will naturally feel superior to the other's feeble attempts to integrate that function. And even if there is a genuine desire to help the other, it can put the other's back up if it is not done in just the right away.

The woman in our story wants to draw this totem god, the buffalo bull, into the ordinary human realm, using him to plow fields and so on, and in this way she helps to destroy it. The food of the husband's tribe is not to be eaten by the bull, so when he eats the peas he becomes visible and is killed by the husband.

The members of the girl's tribe, before killing themselves when they learn of the bull's death, sing the same song she had sung to it, addressing the bull as the Magician of the Plain, born out of the wind, dying before the right time had come, and so on, but the song has lost its power and there is no longer any meaning in their lives.

This woman tried to touch the animus problem too soon. It

was an attempt toward consciousness too early, and therefore took on a negative aspect.

The villagers of her tribe also sing, "He is the one who spreads flowers and fruits on his way"—a description later applied to Osiris, the god who dies too young. This son-god of the Great Mother later becomes the personification of the animus, as in our story, which is typical for an African god.

5
Anima Stories

I will begin with a few primitive examples.

There is a South American story in which a man catches a female ape and takes her into his hut. He discovers while she lives with him that whenever he goes out, by the time he comes back all the work in and around the hut has been done. So one day he decides to find out how that happens, and instead of leaving, he hides and watches.

He sees a beautiful girl appear out of the ape skin, and it is she who does the work. He reaches into the hut and snatches the ape skin and burns it. Then he speaks to the girl and asks her to remain with him. She agrees to stay, on the one condition that he never call her an ape or remind her of her people. He is glad to accept this condition, but there comes a time when his anger is aroused against her over something, and in his fury he calls her an ape. The girl then immediately resumes her ape skin, takes their child—which had been born in the meantime—and runs off. The man is so angry that he burns down his whole hut.

In another story, almost identical, the woman is a female dog, and when the man calls her a bitch she runs away.

Another story, slightly different, concerns a hunter who finds that a jaguar he brings home is a beautiful woman. She agrees to stay with him if he will never betray to his tribe that she is really a jaguar. He promises. But his mother is a persistent, nagging woman who asks indiscreet questions, until at last he tells her the secret. Later, during a festival, his mother gets drunk and tells the whole tribe. Then the girl, "growling from being ashamed," resumes her jaguar shape and disappears forever into the forest.

In still another story, the animal form of the girl is a bee. As long as the husband keeps his promise not to call her "bee," he finds bee-hives wherever he goes in the forest, and he becomes a wealthy man. But when he betrays the secret, he finds no more bee-hives and loses his fortune.

In another tale about an ape woman, the man cuts off the tail, and then keeps the woman under the same condition as in the other stories. One day he sees the family of his wife sitting in the trees and making merry. They invite him to come up and have a drink. The party becomes wild and he gets drunk and tells them that his wife is an ape. Then they and his wife all run away from him—and he is left sitting up in the tree with the problem of how to get down.

All these stories illustrate the primitive attitude that the animal side is also the divine side. A human cannot deal with it; the only thing to do is to accept the animal as a divine and secret mystery, a divine secret. If this attitude is lacking, if there is an attempt to draw the divine into the human realm, there can only be a catastrophe.

But to keep such a secret is absolutely isolating. When the girl in these tales tells the man to keep her identity a secret, she cuts him off from the collective. Generally, even in our society, the secrets leak out, but as long as we keep a secret we are isolated from the general *participation mystique*. That is why there are stories which say that one shouldn't look at the anima or animus—though of course they are not called that—because to look at them is to transcend human boundaries and enter the realm of the divine.

Another such story tells of a young man living in the communal bachelors' hut. Through a hole in the roof he sees a beautiful star, which he watches night after night, until finally he falls in love with it.

One evening he wakes out of his sleep and finds a beautiful woman at the foot of his bed. She says, "You called me." She agrees to live with him, and every night she appears to him as a woman and they have a wonderful time together. During the day, however, she becomes very, very small, so that he can put her in a little bottle, and no one knows her identity. People look into the bottle, but they see only a very disgusting looking animal with mean little eyes. That is, in the banal light of day—to the eyes that see in the daytime—it is all nonsense, but the eyes that see in the night are able to discover the beautiful woman.

For the primitive unconsciousness, this is an intolerable situation—they can't stand the paradox. They have a terrific awe of the unconscious on the one hand, and on the other they have a banal, down-to-earth attitude. Whatever happens is a just-so story. The tension would be too great if they were to try to unite the two aspects: by day, the animal mystery; by night, goddess of the stars.

Continuing this story of the star goddess, the young man is consumed with curiosity about where she goes when she leaves him. Against her warnings, he insists that she take him along the next time. He goes up to heaven with her, and there he sees what she does: she dances among skeletons, and she herself is one. The impact of this discovery is so great that he asks her to let him go back down to earth. She does, but the shock has been too great, and he dies of a brain fever.

That is why the North American Indian stories say, "Don't look up at the stars—they are death and we shouldn't look at them." In some uncanny way, the primitive mind knows they are projections of the unconscious, and we must stay away from them because we haven't the strength to deal with them.

For us who are so cut off from the unconscious it is good to read these stories. Many men and women have chosen not to marry the one they first fell in love with, and then later in analysis this first love appears in dreams as a personification of their anima or animus. Had they married, one can see that it would have been a disaster, creating a lot of difficulties. The unconscious wisdom which prevented them from marrying is the same instinct which drives the primitive to tell such stories and say, "Don't look at the stars."

6
The Black Princess

There are two versions of this European fairy tale which illustrates the dark aspect of the anima. When the anima appears in such a way, we must remember that both versions come from Catholic countries, where the light side of the anima is already recognized and projected onto the Virgin Mary, and so in compensation the emphasis is on the dark side, the black side of the anima.

The Austrian version of "The Black Princess" starts with an old king and queen. The queen desperately wants to have a child, but they had none. A river runs through the town, with a bridge spanning it. On the right side of the bridge is a crucifix, and on the left side a stone figure of Lucifer. (It is common in Europe for a crucifix to stand near bridges in order to protect travelers, because the devil lives under the bridge and tries to pull people under.)

The queen goes regularly to the bridge and cries and prays to Christ to give her a child, but after a while she becomes tired of doing this and getting no results, so she decides to turn to the devil. Then, after three months, she finds herself pregnant.

The king feels that he isn't responsible for this pregnancy, but he says nothing about it. At the end of six months he gives a huge festival, and at the end of nine months the queen gives birth to a coal-black baby girl.

This child grows as much in one hour as any other would in a year, and so in twenty-four hours she is already an adult. At this time she says to the king and the queen, "Oh, you unhappy father and unhappy mother, now I must die. Bury me behind the altar in the church, and always keep a guard in the church during the night, or I will bring a terrible catastrophe on the land."

(The South German parallel of this story says that a witch gives the old couple tea, which makes the queen pregnant with the black child. The witch tells the king to drink it "in the name of God," but the king is so excited that he blurts out: "in the name of God and the Devil." The black child is born, and calls, "Father." The king answers, "Yes, my child." She replies, "Now I have talked for the first time." This happens three times, after which she says, "I have talked for the third time. Now make an iron coffin, because I must die," giving instructions as in the other version for her burial behind the altar and for the guard.)

And so the black woman is buried behind the altar, and every night a soldier guards the coffin. But every morning when they open the church at 4:00 a.m., they find that the guard has been torn to pieces.

Naturally the people strongly resist being drafted to stand guard in the church, only to be torn to bits, and they come near to starting a revolution because they don't want to serve. And so the king finally brings a regiment of soldiers in from a foreign country where what happens in the church is not known.

Among the foreign regiment there are three brothers, one a major, one a captain, and the third a common soldier who is apparently never going to amount to anything: he lives light heartedly, carouses and spends his money freely, frequently getting into trouble and serving time in prison.

When it is the major's turn to serve as guard, he tricks this common-soldier brother into taking his place. The soldier goes into the church, prays first, and then goes into the pulpit, making crosses on all the steps leading up to it.

At midnight the black woman comes out of her coffin, enveloped in fiery flames. She flies into a rage when she finds him in the pulpit, but she can't climb the steps to reach him because of the crosses. She goes mad trying to get to him, overthrowing the seats, throwing down the statues, even stacking up chairs near the pulpit, trying to reach him. But he is saved because the clock strikes twelve, at which time she must return to her coffin.

The next morning the people are astonished to find the soldier alive. They tell him that since he is so clever, he had better stand guard again the next night. But he is afraid. It seems to him that he has done enough and he tries to escape. While he is trying to get away, he meets an old beggarman who tells him to go back and stand guard, but this time to hide behind the statue of the Virgin Mary.

The soldier does as he is advised, and this time the black princess is even more enraged. It takes her a long time to find where he is hiding, but then just as she is about to catch him the clock strikes twelve and he is saved as before.

The people rejoice to find the soldier alive again the next morning, and now, naturally, he is elected to return for a third night. Again he wants to run away, but again the old beggar intervenes, telling him that this time he should climb into her coffin as soon as she leaves it. He must lie there with his eyes closed, as if he were dead, and make no answer when she discovers him. The old man says the princess will be alarmed when he doesn't get out—she will shout at him, rant and rave; then she will beg him, but only when she says in just the right way, "Rudolph, get up," should he come out of the coffin.

The soldier does as he is told. When the princess quiets down, she turns into a white maiden, and in the morning when the church is opened the two lovers are found. They marry, and later he becomes a king.

(In the other version, it is God, not an old beggar, who intervenes—God becomes tired of all these tricks of Lucifer's daughter; he can't stand them anymore and teaches the soldier how to redeem her.)

*

The story of the black princess has a compensatory function for the modern Christian man. It is the modern situation of the anima problem.

The anima in fairy tales is very often represented as the devil's daughter. This is because the feminine principle in Protestant countries is lacking: there is no goddess, and so she has fallen into the unconscious where she takes on a dark aspect. So in Protestant countries it is the entire anima which is lacking, but in Catholic countries only the dark side is missing, for the Virgin Mary represents the light side.

In the thirteenth century the introduction of the cult of Mary gave the Christian man an idealized feminine figure onto which to project his anima. That is fine as far as it goes, but it had the disadvantage that the individual choice of an anima projection was gone—there was only the single identical anima for every man. In the days of chivalry, each knight chose to serve a particular lady. Then, as Christianity and the cult of Mary took hold, there came the increasing persecution of witches as men experienced the fascination of a specific woman.

You see, the element of reality carried by an individual woman is not represented in the goddess or in an ideal figure such as the Virgin Mary. To put together all these paradoxical aspects of the feminine, and to know how to relate to them, is one of the great difficulties.

The initial situation in "The Black Princess" is that the king and queen have no children. This means that the ruling attitude, personified in the king, has become sterile. Though there is a balance between the masculine and feminine powers, the situation lacks new life—perhaps because darkness is excluded. The queen wants desperately to have a child, and that is why she eventually prays to Lucifer when she has had enough of praying to Christ without result.

In a similar Austrian tale, the devil has a wife who is also his grandmother, and at the same time he has a daughter who lives with them. Thus there is an incestuous relationship. So we have the double set-up:

in the Christian religion:	God	Son	Holy Ghost
and below:	Devil	Grandmother	Daughter

The general Christian way of thinking is that the Holy Ghost is a necessity for humanity. It enters us and enables us to do things even beyond Christ. In the dark side, it is the devil's daughter who has the true feeling for mankind, who loves men. This devil's daughter is the link between the dark side and the light.

In our story the king feels that he isn't responsible for the pregnancy; it is really Lucifer who has impregnated the queen. There are medieval legends that the devil will have a daughter and will commit incest with her, and her child will become the Anti-Christ.

There is the queer fact that the devil's daughter, the Black Princess, grows so quickly: she speaks only three times, and she grows as much in one hour as a natural child does in a year. This characterizes her as being inhuman, with magic powers, living outside the human world of time and space.

We are in the habit of speaking of the unconscious as having no time and space boundaries, and because we ourselves are imprisoned in time and space, we cannot understand the unconscious. But this tale tells us that the archetypes in the unconscious cannot understand our life either, because they live *outside* time and space, that is, in another rhythm of life.

So the black princess lives life in a different rhythm, which probably refers to a fact that we observe in everyday life—that the anima in anima-possessed men acts on age levels quite unconnected with the actual age of the man himself, and *her* timelessness prevents him from getting into the "here" and, especially, the "now" of the present moment. There is always the anima outside time, pulling the man outside time, disturbing the whole normal rhythm of his development. Then you have these "wise" young boys and "childish" old men.

In the story she appears in fiery flames, too full of uncontrolled energy and libido, destroying life. She represents a vitality which doesn't carry a man into life, but somehow carries him outside of life. (In the German parallel, she doesn't tear the men to pieces, she eats them. She is always hungry.)

This anima contains the element of impatience that you find in anima-possessed men: their unwillingness or refusal to do what is necessary right now, at this moment. That is also seen in the fast growth of the black princess, because she is living in this unnatural rhythm. She belongs to eternity and to the gods, and it is illegitimate to pull her into human areas of life.

Three times she calls, "Father," and then she says, "Now I will die and you must bury me behind the altar; and every night there must be a guard in the church."

Here she reveals who she really is—what she really represents—namely, the shadow of the prevailing Christian dogma. She is *behind* the altar, the shadow side; she makes known who she is by asking to be buried there. One could say that she has taken a step toward her redemption by revealing her divine nature, dark as it is.

Regarding the iron coffin, iron is the metal of the planet Mars and is associated with the god of the same name. Iron has to do with conflict, because Mars is the god of war. Also, in alchemical writings it refers to the mortal, decaying body, because iron rusts so easily. Therefore it comes to represent the decaying mortal matter of the body, that aspect of our nature which is corruptible. This meaning probably derives from the Biblical reference to treasures which rust cannot eat. [Matt. 6:19]

The black princess is now imprisoned in the iron coffin, which reflects the fact that what we reject psychologically often becomes imprisoned in the body. She is dead during the day, but alive at night, which shows the shadowy aspect of this anima figure. In just this way, men may be unconscious of the influence of their anima during their daytime life, and then be assailed by her at night, in dreams.

Now she starts to kill human beings, and threatens to bring about a catastrophe in the land. For the most part, she destroys simple men, namely soldiers—not the rulers, but the simple people—which shows how the anima attacks the emotional side, the side of the inferior function.[15] On the collective level, we see this occur in so-called populist movements, such as Communism or Nazism, where this aspect of anima possession is at work.

In fairy tales it is typically the "inferior" man, the fool or dummling, who redeems the princess. Here he is a light-hearted spendthrift, drinking too much and ending up in jail. But he has the ability to redeem the princess. He becomes the great hero because he is naive and not afraid of the dark. The naive one has the gift of being spontaneous and the ability to expose oneself to new facts; that is the proper attitude toward the unconscious.

On the first night, the young soldier climbs up into the pulpit, making little crosses on the steps. And the second night, he hides behind the Virgin Mary. Thus twice he escapes by climbing up.

The first escape is very subtle: he goes to where the priest

---

[15] [See below, pp. 86ff.—Ed.]

talks to the community; that is how he saves himself. Though the priest usually carries a collective role as a spiritual leader, here the soldier is taking the priest's role as a leader of the collective, the teacher and truth-teller to the community. He takes on this role of one who knows and leads, in order not to be overcome by the unconscious. There is a hint here that one way a man can deal with the anima is not to become overwhelmed and simply passive, but rather to try to take action in some way.

The real essence of a priest is that he has renounced the experience of the anima in its earthly aspect, that is, through an actual woman, and he keeps himself above the situation as much as he can. At all costs, he must keep his head and not be overrun.

Of course, this only puts off the solution for our hero; it is a temporary solution, too near the old attitude to be the final answer. It is a form of escape—but then, for a soldier to play the role of a priest means he is trying to get above the situation. We say in German that intellectuals "dance up and down with their brain." If we ask, "Why don't they ever come down to earth, touch earth?" the answer is that they fear the black anima will get them.

Sometimes, for the time being, nothing else can be done. This is at least a putting off of the problem. The pulpit also represents that part which is relatively intellectual. It is only a putting off, because the fiery black princess pulls up chairs and would have got him except that midnight comes. This does indicate that she is bound to a certain time rhythm here, and appears in that time rhythm. She is bound—and not bound.

That is the great problem with the unconscious. It is only a *relative* time and *relative* space. The unconscious is not completely outside time. As the figure of a human person, the princess has come into the human realm to this extent. The striking of the clock, or the crowing of the cock, which ends her activity for the night, may be connected with the turn toward morning, when consciousness begins increasing again.

One could say that the anima is also affected by the fact that if a man tries to relate to her, the poor girl becomes bound to the human. Animus and anima are not always happy to have this relationship—they lose part of their power when they are made conscious. They would prefer to remain gods and goddesses and keep their power. That is why there is a certain amount of energetic resistance to their integration.

This cage of time and space can also be helpful. In the case of the clock striking midnight, the soldier is saved by time. Thus, a man should fight his impatience, which is an anima trick. He should accept the boundaries of time and space. If he would take the attitude that this is a helpful thing, this prison of time and space, then just waiting, putting off, using time as an element, sometimes helps to bring about an increase in consciousness.

When a man is possessed by the anima, then he feels that he must *immediately* do something about the situation—it is terribly urgent to send off a letter, for instance, or telephone and speak his mind. The tip-off to this state of possession is often just this feeling of urgency that it has to be done *this minute.*

There are stories among primitive tribes and in northern Europe which revolve around a competition as to who can annoy the opponent into exploding first. The one who endures the annoying and tormenting the longest without losing control of his temper wins the contest, and the loser must become his servant, obliged to do the most demeaning things. But this servant plays his tricks too, and one day the other will explode, and then the servant can cut off his head!

If one doesn't allow such a panic or rush to get the better of oneself, then the figure in the unconscious will begin to change. This happens in our story when the soldier gets into the coffin and plays dead; he won't listen or answer or pay any attention to the black princess's threats.

I know an analyst whose patient came to say good-bye, since he intended to commit suicide immediately afterward. She didn't discuss his decision with him—she couldn't have answered the threat directly—but just persuaded him to first drink a glass of wine with her . . . and another . . . and another. Thus time intervened and the suicide didn't happen.

If one can contain the excitement, delay acting on it, one finally becomes tired, which is a good way of dealing with such a destructive emotional outburst. Therefore time is a terribly important factor in dealing with the anima.

Next time the soldier wants to run away because he thinks he has done enough, but he meets the old man (or, in the German tale, God, who is fed up with the devil's tricks) who tells him to climb up behind the Virgin Mary. This is the place of the shadowy, dark aspect of the feminine, the aspect that has not been included in the collective. When he goes there, it is already the same thing as later when he gets into her coffin. That is, he takes her place away from her, as though saying, "I know you, know where you belong, where you come from."

A man threatened by the anima can become conscious by going into the place where the anima is, and then resisting her. This is a double trick, to follow the fascination and at the same time to deal with it. Some men always try to escape when they see the anima situation coming up; or else they say, "To hell with it," and go straight into it. But to go into it without *falling* into it, that is the difficult thing. It is a slap in the face to the usual male attitude, because it goes against the grain.

A man wants something to be either *this* or *that,* not be so paradoxical. Following the fascination but dealing with it at the same time is *not* the puer aeternus situation, where the attitude is to have the whole experience, but not to commit to anything.[16] Rather it is the struggle for the light and the search for meaning, which require the man to assume moral responsibility.

In the animus situation, his destructiveness takes the form of an inner argument, which makes it necessary to give him something to chew on. But for a man, if he goes into a place where the anima herself is, it would mean that here he takes a step into life. This has to do with the fact that the anima is an archetype of life, and the animus an archetype of death.

There is a Gypsy romance in which a woman marries Death. He disappears from time to time, and she begs him to tell her where he goes. He tells her she wouldn't be able to face it, but she wears him down and he finally reveals himself as Death. The shock of this discovery kills her. While he stayed with the woman, Death would forget to kill people on the earth, and then the people would multiply until there were too many. It is necessary that he perform his duties as Death.

In the human realm, men do the actual work of death in the outer world, as hunters and warriors, etc., while women do the work of life, giving and preserving it. That is why it reverses itself on the inside—why animus possession makes a woman fall out of real life, while a man possessed by the anima gets entangled in it. The anima's darkness is that she wants to entangle the man in the doubtful ambiguities of life, while the dark side of the animus is a demon who would pull women away from life, cut them off from it. So the man must take a step into real life, into the dark side, in the place where the anima is. In the case of the woman, she must run away and not step into death.

Naturally, these comments refer to this particular story: if the anima appears like this, as a dark power, and sleeps like this in

---

[16] [See von Franz, *The Problem of the Puer Aeternus,* esp. pp. 8ff.—Ed.]

an iron coffin, then we must say that the man will not get away without doing certain things in life. It is from the hint of darkness and fire that we must conclude that he must step into life. This compensates Christian consciousness, where very often a man doesn't want to step into a situation because he might get some spots on his lily-white shirt.

The third night, the soldier actually has to go into the black princess's coffin. The coffin has to do with the place where the dead body, the corpse, lives—it is a rejection of the physical. In the Christian dogma, it is the rejection of the "natural man."

The general attitude in Christian countries considers the body to be sinful, and so it is rejected. That is why here he must step in, realize what she wants. He goes into the coffin, shuts his eyes and doesn't move. He goes through a symbolic death. He lets himself be symbolically killed. He must give up completely in order that the anima can show a different aspect.

7
The Virgin Czarina

"The Virgin Czarina" is a Russian story where the dark and light aspects of the anima are linked.[17] Fairy tales are an expression of the collective unconscious; thus an overemphasis on the dark side has to do with the fact that they are compensating a too-light attitude in collective consciousness.

A czar had three sons, two of them intelligent, but the third one was very silly, generally drunk and thoroughly despised by everyone. The czar had become old. One night, at a dinner party with his generals, he gave a speech in which he said, "I wonder which one of my three sons will pick my flowers and follow in my footsteps?"

The eldest son, Teodor, said, "Father, give me your blessing and permission to pluck your flowers and follow in your footsteps, and I will try." The czar was pleased and commanded that he be given the best horse in the stables. It was saddled and bridled and the brave lad rode out into the open country.

After some distance he came to a crossroads, where a sign read: "He who takes the road to the right will get plenty of food but his horse will remain hungry; he who rides to the left, his horse will find food but he himself will go hungry; he who rides on the middle road will suffer death."

After considering awhile, Teodor decided to take the road to the right. This road led him to a mountain which he climbed, and there at the top he found a brass snake. He picked it up and brought it back to court to present to his father.

---

[17] [A more elaborate version of this story, though essentially the same, appears in Reinhold Olesch, ed., *Russian Folktales*, pp. 119ff.—Ed.]

Upon seeing the snake, the czar was thrown into consternation and cried, "What the hell have you brought here! This is a horrible thing—it will destroy our whole empire!" In a rage he threw the boy into prison.

Sometime later, in a better mood, the czar was again at dinner with his generals, and again asked the question: "I wonder which one of my three sons will pick my flowers and follow in my footsteps?"

Dimitri, the second son, said, "Father, I will try."

So he takes the best horse in the stables and rides out. He too comes to the crossroads and reads the same sign: "He who takes the road to the right will get plenty of food but his horse will remain hungry; he who rides to the left, his horse will find food but he himself will go hungry; he who rides on the middle road will suffer death."

He thinks, "Well, if my horse is well fed, he will find the way. I will take the left road."

The road leads him eventually to a house with golden columns. Inside, he finds an attractive woman lying in a great bed which continually turns round and round. He promptly gets into bed with her—but she presses a button and he is dropped into the cellar, where he finds a lot of other men who have gone before him. There he is stuck, and never goes home.

The czar is very sad for a long time at the disappearance of his son. But eventually he organizes another feast and muses again to his generals: "I wonder which one of my three sons will pick my flowers and follow in my footsteps?"

His third son Ivan, the idiot-hero, speaks up: "Father, I would like to try."

The czar ridicules him, saying, "You?—you are completely unable; you can only sit on the stove, that's all you can do."

Ivan answers, "Father, with or without your blessing and permission, I will go."

So the czar commands that he be given the best horse. But in the stable there is a small, almost worn-out mare, the worst horse of all, used only for carrying water to the court. Ivan gets on her, facing the tail, and the whole town laughs at him, calling him a simpleton as he starts out on his journey.

Ivan comes to the same crossroads as his brothers, and reads the same sign: "He who takes the road to the right will get plenty of food but his horse will remain hungry; he who rides to the left, his horse will find food but he himself will go hungry; he who rides on the middle road will suffer death."

The boy begins to weep, saying, "Oh, am I not a poor fellow that I will have to die!" But he starts down the road that leads straight ahead, pulling so violently on the horse's bridle that he takes off the whole skin of the horse. He hangs it on a post, saying to a crow nearby, "There you are, crow—now you will have something to eat!"

Then he roars like an animal and whistles like a dragon. A fiery horse appears. From its mouth blaze flames, from its nostrils flash sparks, from its ears rise steam, and fiery apples shoot out of its behind! Ivan takes this steed by the bridle and strokes it until it is calm.

Before continuing his journey, Ivan goes down into his grandfather's cellar where he eats a lot to strengthen himself. His grandfather (apparently a ghost, an ancestral spirit) gives him a beautiful saddle and whip for his horse, and teaches him how to tame and control the horse.

Ivan then jumps on the horse and rides until he comes to a little hut which stands on chicken legs and continually rotates like a spindle. He sings out, "Little hut, stand still, turn your face to the woods and answer me!"

Then he sees the old witch, Baba Yaga, combing yarn with a

long finger, scratching in the ashes with her long nose, and watching with glittering eyes the geese in the field.

She says to him, "Tell me, child, do you come here voluntarily or involuntarily?"

Ivan answers, "Shut up, you old witch! You shouldn't question a hero. Bring me something to eat and drink or I'll chop off your ears and knock off your head, and sand will come out of your arse!"

She then serves him a beautiful supper, and he asks her, "Has my father ever come this way?"

"Yes," she says, and then he asks her the way to the virgin czarina, Maria with the golden tresses. She can't give him this information, but tells him to travel on till he meets her sister, and to ask her the way.

He goes on to the second witch, who also asks him, "Do you come here voluntarily or involuntarily?"

He shouts at her as he did with the first witch, and again is served a good meal. She too says yes, his father has passed this way. He asks her how to reach the virgin czarina, but she says he will have to go on to the third witch who will tell him the way.

This third witch, after being threatened as before and serving him food and drink, tells him he will have to go to the Kingdom Under the Sun, where he will find a beautiful garden. In this garden are the rejuvenating apples, and there he will also find the waters of life and death. Nearby is the castle of the virgin czarina, Maria with the golden tresses, who rules the Kingdom Under the Sun.

Ivan travels on until he comes to a great town. He finds the rejuvenating apples, and the two wells, the waters of life and death. He takes a great crow and tears it to pieces, and then sprinkles water from each well on it. When he sprinkles it with the water of death, it disappears; when he sprinkles it with the water of life, it comes back to life. In this way he finds out for himself which is the water of life.

Now he goes on to the castle of Maria, taking with him the rejuvenating apples and a vial of each kind of water. He finds the virgin czarina asleep. She is beautiful beyond all belief, and quite transparent, so that he can see her heart and the marrow flowing in her bones. He rapes her as she sleeps and quietly leaves before she wakens.

Ivan is terribly exhausted now, and his horse, too, is nearly dead with weariness. But he sprinkles it with some of the water of life, and they hurry on.

In the meantime, Maria with the golden tresses has woken up, and is furious that a thief has been in her garden. She takes off in pursuit of the boy, and he flees before her. In jumping over a wall, the left hind foot of his horse strikes a little bell—Maria has such hidden bells all over the town to sound the alarm against intruders. All the people in the town wake up and race after him, led by Maria.

Ivan's flight back leads past the huts of the three witches, and each one in turn calls out to Maria as she appears in pursuit: "Oh, Maria, come on in and have a cup of tea—you can catch that idiot later." Maria stops in with each of them, thus giving him a chance to escape again. He comes to the crossroads before her, and there she has to turn back.

But Ivan himself now turns back too, for he has an impulse to look for his brother Dimitri who never returned. He finds the house of the woman with the turning bed and gets in with her, but he presses the button first, and she falls down into the cellar with all the previous would-be lovers, who tear her to pieces.

Ivan then frees them all, including his brother. Now he is so exhausted that he goes to sleep. Dimitri steals the rejuvenating apples and the waters of life and death, and takes them back to the court, saying he is the one who found them. When Ivan returns home, he doesn't say anything about his adventures or Dimitri's deception.

A year later, a ship draws up near the town, carrying Maria herself, the virgin with the golden tresses. She shoots off big cannons and muskets against the court, demanding the father of her two sons, *at once*. The czar looks out at the bombardment. He is puzzled—who is the guilty one? The shooting continues and the situation becomes crucial. Finally Teodor, the eldest son, goes out to the ship, but Maria sends out her slaves who beat him back. Dimitri then tries and gets the same treatment. She still demands the guilty one, the father of her two sons.

Everyone is wondering. Then one of the generals says, "Ivan is always going around in the inns, getting drunk and telling funny stories. Let's try him."

They find Ivan in his dirty and rumpled uniform, half drunk, and send him out to meet Maria. Her two sons immediately run out to meet him, shouting "Father!"—and they take him by the hand and all go into the ship.

Since Maria is very powerful, the czar now changes his attitude toward Ivan, and offers him the whole kingdom of Russia. But Ivan says, "No, thank you," and he sails away with Maria and the two boys into the Kingdom Under the Sun.

*

This story begins with the quaternity of four figures (like the story of the little magic horse, where there were first the king and his daughter, and the Div and the horse). There is no mention of the queen, so the feminine is missing.

Here we have the czar, Teodor, Dimitri—and then Ivan, the fourth. Ivan comes to the crossroads as his brothers had before him. On one side is a road that leads to the mountain with the brass snake; on the other side is a road that will take him to the house of the whore with the turning bed. Going straight ahead—where it is said he will suffer death—he comes to another quaternity: three similar witches, and the fourth one is Maria (they are all one family, you see: three aunts and a niece).

In each quaternity it is the fourth one who is the uniting factor. The end result of the story is that the old court is still left with no feminine principle, and the youngest son, the new life, is lacking. That is, the situation is destroyed in its totality. And on the other side, in the Kingdom Under the Sun, we have the quaternity of Maria, Ivan and the two sons.

The beginning quaternity (in the court) is completely masculine, and the compensating quaternity (the three witches and Maria) is completely feminine. The end situation in the Kingdom Under the Sun contains at least one feminine figure, so that is an advance.

The story opens with the familiar theme of the old king who is worn out. The two eldest brothers are opposites: one of them goes too much to the right, upward; the other goes too much to the left, downward. One starves the horse, going astray into the upper realm of the intellectual; the other starves himself but feeds the horse, giving in too much to the instincts, to the animal. The third son, Ivan, who goes straight ahead, "dies" between the opposites.

Presumably the czar was once the lover of Maria too, given his own words: "Follow in my footsteps and pick my flowers." But now he is old.

The czar represents a dominant collective attitude which was once near the well of life, that is, close to the psychic flow in the unconscious. Through growing old, this collective dominant has lost contact with its unconscious sources. The king then is no longer a symbol of the Self, but has become representative of a worn-out collective ruling system.

So the king puts it to the generals in his court: which of his three sons can go back to the source of life, where at one time he was himself? His directive to "pick my flowers" has erotic connotations. So, though it may be squeezing too much meaning out of that phrase, perhaps it is not too much to assume that the czar himself is the father of the sons of Maria, that in his younger days the czar flirted with her—a mother anima in the daughter aspect.

The description of the court makes us think of Jung's model of typology and the four functions.[18] The czar represents the developed or superior function, now worn out, no longer in connection with the inner psychic life. He has two sons, the auxiliary functions, which are opposite to each other, and then there is Ivan, whose undisciplined behavior is similar to that typically associated with the inferior function.[19]

But we have already said that the czar represents a ruling collective attitude, so can we also consider the court set-up as a pattern of the four functions? Yes. Though the four functions only apply to actual human beings, we *can* talk about a pattern of functions which is inherent in the human psyche.

It is quite possible to draw certain deductions about a person when you know that person's type. There are patterns. No matter what the inferior function might be, it is always linked with emotions; it is always a handicap in the outer world; it is always linked with the mystical. This typical characteristic of the inferior function can be deduced because there *is* a pattern in the human psyche.

So we can say that the czar's court shows a basic pattern on

---

[18] [See *Psychological Types*, CW 6, par. 731; also Daryl Sharp, *Personality Types: Jung's Model of Typology*, esp. pp. 12ff.—Ed.]

[19] [For more detailed commentary, see "The Inferior Function," in Marie-Louise von Franz and James Hillman, *Lectures on Jung's Typology.*—Ed.]

which the four functions of a human being develop. It is a pattern of the conscious world, while Maria and her three witchy aunts would be the pattern of the unconscious world, seen from a masculine angle.

The interesting thing in this story is that the main function—the czar—doesn't do much harm to Ivan. The czar simply despises him, with the attitude, "You're hopeless." That is typical of the ego's attitude toward the inferior function.

But the two older brothers are disturbing factors. Dimitri is even dangerous to Ivan, stealing his treasures. The two are doubtful figures because, although they reflect the pattern of the auxiliary functions, at the same time they represent what is meant by the expression, "neither fish nor fowl."

The superior function, for instance, may manifest in an outstanding personality. Then the inferior function will be fairly limited, but it will have all the mystical qualities usually associated with the inferior function, enabling the individual to turn to the field of the unconscious. This is a bad thing only when it is turned toward the outside world. The two auxiliary functions are just average, not outstanding in any way, and just so, it is the *average* personality that can be the greatest disturbance in an individual's adventure—it doesn't want to risk itself.

Ivan's brothers want security—they don't want to go down the path that leads to death. The czar has been there; he is not a coward. And Ivan goes, for he is not a coward either. But these two brothers, who stand for the reluctant, undifferentiated, average person, are dangerous enemies of the hero. They don't go as far as the main one, the superior function, and they won't take the risks of the inferior function.

At first they are differentiated—one brother goes to the mountain, and the other, in a silly sense, falls into the animal instincts (the whore's cellar). But when they become constellated—after the second auxiliary becomes developed—then there is too great a weight on the conscious side. Consciousness becomes very strong, and that is a moment of danger, where too great a split from the unconscious may occur, because the ego has so much power. Tension arises with the development of the third function, and this tension is not relieved because the fourth is undeveloped and therefore cannot provide a balance.

The fourth function is less concrete than the others; it conveys an experience on the symbolic level, while the others convey it either in an intellectual way or in an experiential way. Thus, from the perspective of consciousness, it seems like an inner death to risk sacrificing the security of the concrete.

In the field of consciousness, there is always an "inner" and an "outer"—the concrete or the symbolic, the spiritual or the physical—but the fourth function generally leads into a reality where this split does not exist. That is, the anxious question of the ego—"Which is *real?*"—is not there. This is intolerable from the standpoint of consciousness. Therefore, a symbolic death is necessary in order for the inferior function to develop.

Let us consider the symbolism of the brass snake. In the Bible, Moses lifted up the brass snake before the people of Israel in order to free them from a certain evil. [Num. 21:9] The Church Fathers have always interpreted this as a prefiguration of Christ, as did the Gnostics. It possessed the highest saving qualities. But in our story the czar is horrified. "Don't bring this monster into our kingdom," he says, "it will destroy everything!"

This shows how any symbol may in time become one-sided and destructive. That which has once been a saving factor—the lifting up of the serpent into the spiritual realm—this symbolic gesture, which was emphasized in Christianity as it also was in earlier times, has now lost its redemptive qualities and has become destructive.

Dimitri followed the road which led only into the instinctual experience, without the inclusion of the spiritual. Teodor took the other road and found the brass snake. Brass is an alloy of copper and zinc. Copper belongs to the planet Venus, the goddess of love, and the ordinary Aphrodite. So Teodor falls into the opposite aspect of Aphrodite—it is sublime but it is dead!

Both the older brothers are looking for the anima. They both find something that has to do with Venus, but each finds it in too one-sided a way. This would be like trying to experience love as something only symbolic. A person lands in the cellar, in a collective, among a lot of other fellows who fell into the same blind trap. A cellar means darkness; one is enclosed in the darkness of the instinctive drive and its collective elements, all because one had not the courage to say: "I just don't know which way it is. Let me simply go where I must."

Ivan doesn't behave like a hero going to his death. He is completely human and bursts into tears of despair. He is an ordinary human being, naturally unhappy about having to die. This natural, spontaneous, ordinary human being is the one chosen to be the hero. He is typical of the hero of that time, compensating for the knightly ideal peculiar to Christian countries. It has only been since the era of the Christian knight and the aristocratic English gentleman that the natural man has been rejected. This may have led to the development of the spiritual, but it splits people from the ordinary human being.

Ivan takes with him the little horse whose previous function was to carry water. The little horse (the instincts) is still alive, but worn out. Ivan symbolically asks himself, "What will best carry me?" and answers, "That which works for the collective unconscious will best carry me." The little mare carried into the court the living powers of the psyche, symbolized by water.

People in analysis often ask, "Where shall I start in active imagination?" I say, "One must start where there is still a flow of energy, even if it is just a thin flow, even if it seems silly." Ivan is the natural man, so he spontaneously chooses the right horse. But he sits on it the wrong way around, with his horse looking in the right direction and himself looking back toward the town. Everybody laughs at him—but in the end he is the one who saves the situation.

This is a subtle symbolic motif: as long as we point our inferior function in the same direction as that of consciousness, it is just a fool. Feeling in a thinking-type man will be heavy, slow, mystical, inarticulate, as long he looks at it from the viewpoint of his extraverted thinking. He will be afraid to trust his feeling, afraid he would just make a complete mess of his life. He must realize that although his other functions may be well developed, in the use of his inferior function he is just a school boy.

Many people try to turn their inferior function in the same direction as their conscious interests take them. If they are extraverted, they try to develop their feeling function, say, toward the outside world also. Similarly, the introvert cannot work everything out on the inside. It is absolutely important that the introvert work out a relationship with the inferior function in the outside world, just as the extravert must recognize the inferior function in the inner world.

Thus, the inferior function of feeling, for instance, not only *looks* foolish, it *is* foolish. But as soon as it faces toward its own realm, it is no longer foolish. The inferior function has the ability to become the connection between the unconscious and the outer world. In the realm of the ruling function, it is just foolish, awkward, making one ridiculous, childish, silly.

Ivan has no doubts about taking the path straight ahead—and that is one of the principal qualities of the inferior function. With a natural, instinctive knowledge, he is sure that he has to go straight ahead, though it seems that the path leads to death. There is a completely simple straightforwardness about the inferior function; it is not sophisticated or argumentative, it simply wants to break through. If it is turned in the right direction, it is no longer awkward and foolish but leads to the goal.

The path straight ahead from the crossroads leads to the realm of the three witches, and then on to Maria with the golden tresses. From such a structure in the unconscious, this means crucifixion, death. Like the simple soldier in "The Black Princess," Ivan has to enter the coffin, a voluntary form of death. As soon as he has passed the crossroads, this dangerous point, he pulls at the bridle of the little mare and tears off its skin. He throws it to the crows, saying, "There, you can eat it!" Then he whistles, and the magic horse comes.

The new horse is like a transformation of the old horse that was killed. Ivan discards the old horse and gains a new one; or, one could say, through the killing of the old one it is revived in a new form. He sort of turns the old horse inside out (tearing off its skin), and then what looked so miserable before becomes the fiery, heroic horse.

First, Ivan turns himself—he had started out looking regressively toward the world he was leaving, instead of looking forward to the unknown, but later he turned around—and then he forces the horse that carried him to make the same change.

A feeling-type man may complain that he just gets too tired, he has no libido, when he tries to force himself to read. "I would like to do it," he says, "but I just haven't the strength." But his whole approach is from the wrong direction; he is looking at the thing with worldly eyes, as if he were a schoolboy confronted by a textbook. If he could turn this attitude around by saying, "Well, I do think in a foolish way, but let me really think just what I think, and not mind if it's silly." If he would then go on with it, he might suddenly become deeply fascinated by what he reads. It is only when he is looking at the matter with conventional eyes that there is no energy for it.

Feeling types have an enormous philosophical thinking, which is not thinking as we learn it at school. It has the gush of energy that characterized early Greek thinking—an unspoiled kind of thinking which dares to ask the questions that the sophisticated thinker has lost the power to ask. When someone can do this— think naively—then generally there is a sudden transformation of libido, such as represented in our fairy tale by this miserable little mare turning into the heroic golden horse that carries Ivan into the most amazing new experiences.

This happens only by turning the inside outside in the human part of the function, and even in the instinctive part of the function. It is naturally a sacrifice, with all the painful implications of a sacrifice, because one has to give up mapping out or programming what one thinks.

When you try to teach people how to develop their inferior function, they generally agree with the experiment, but they want to map it out with the main function, to decide where it has to go—a sort of patronizing of the inferior function. When the inferior function starts to work on its own initiative, it is experienced by the personality as a crucifixion, a symbolic death.

An extravert once came to me for analysis. He had overused his intuition in a most successful but at the same time a most destructive way, so that his whole physical makeup practically gave out. He had become impotent sexually, so in analysis his amazing extraverted intuition (his excellent dog-nose) ran ahead, sorting through the possibilities. He decided that to be cured of his impotence, the best thing would be for him to fall in love. That would be the answer. But then he fell in love with a woman whom he couldn't possibly get, for outer reasons.

It was a devilish trick of the unconscious to put him in a situation like this, up against a wall. His dreams would not let him get away without accepting this fact. If he tried to win the woman, as his unconscious seemed to insist, it looked like a sure catastrophe. It was an impossible situation and could only lead to disappointment. Yet his unconscious finally impelled him to try. It was a shattering experience, but through the shock of it there came up in him an introverted feeling attitude toward her— which cured his impotence. Then he realized how real is inner reality, that it could even cure him. Naturally, he had wanted to map out his course in an extraverted way, but that didn't work.

Had this man been an introvert, the pattern of the cure would have been the opposite: it would have had to be worked out in an extraverted way in the outer world. When the main function is exhausted, the inferior function reveals its mystical aspect, in the sense of something shocking, not understandable from the conscious standpoint. That is a terrible, terrific moment.

The inferior function has also the naiveté to be courageous in facing such a situation, to risk without hope. The effect in our tale is that after the transformation of the horse Ivan goes into the grandfather's cellar. This is typical of what you find in many primitive initiation ceremonies: before setting out on a great adventure, they integrate the ancestral souls. They must unite themselves; otherwise these inherited elements would work in a destructive way later.

There is an Eskimo initiation story about an orphan boy who is rejected by everyone, so that he has to live alone at the very edge of the village. One day he hears a voice and goes out into the snow to see who it is. It is a bear, who says to him: "If your have the courage to stand while I beat you, you will become a great medicine man."

The boy stands and is beaten nearly to death. All during the beating, tiny bon-bons fall out of him until finally there are none left. After this, he goes out into the world and becomes a healer. The name of the bear in this story is "The Great Ancestor."

The beating means both a uniting of oneself and, at the same time, a getting out of one's system things which do not belong there. Sometimes we have picked up particles of the milieu, our surroundings, which do not belong to us personally; therefore we must integrate the ancestors, but sweat out what isn't ours. There is the same significance in those primitive rites where medicine men insert power stones into the body of the new shaman. There are parts of the personality which do not really belong, and other parts which do belong and should be integrated.

Down in his grandfather's cellar, Ivan eats and drinks, which is to say that from the ancestral powers he ingests the means of taming the instincts, the horse.

Question: How does it look, from the standpoint of an introvert, that the inferior function links up with the outer world, when at the same time it leads into the unconscious?

This is subtle, but one can say that it is a symbolic experience of the unconscious *but* linked with the outer object. The outer object cannot be scratched out by the introvert.

This can be illustrated by the experience of a famous French poet who fell hopelessly in love with a common little *midi-nette*.[20] He experienced her as a goddess and wrote poems about her as his Beatrice. Then, with his very French intellectual attitude, he couldn't stand the paradox that she was just an ordinary woman. He decided to keep the relationship completely inside and have nothing more to do with the woman herself. He cut off the relationship, not being able to stand the paradox. But then

---

[20] [The poet is identified as Gérard de Nerval in von Franz's lengthier comments in *Apuleius' Golden Ass*, pp. 82f.—Ed.]

he began having psychotic episodes. He had a dream that he found her in a garden, but she was a statue, broken in two, the upper part of her body lying on the ground. His soul had died from an inner split. In the end, he actually hanged himself.

This is an extreme case of trying to work out everything inside, and in doing so losing the opportunity for individuation. He tried to exclude the outer object from his inner experience. It was both an ordinary love affair and a mystical experience, and he just could not put the two together. Interestingly, during his psychotic phases, whenever he traveled in Germany—and especially in the Black Forest—he always felt all right. Perhaps that is because Germany is (or was then) the land of romanticism.

Question: Can you explain the significance of the third or auxiliary function?

Well, when the primary function is well developed, generally one of the auxiliary functions helps it along; this second function tones the main function. For example, we speak of thinking colored by intuition. If the thinking is more accurate, we have a scientific perspective—that is, thinking colored by an auxiliary sensation function.

Thinking and feeling are rational functions; sensation and intuition are irrational functions. A rational function cannot work on its own. A thinker, for instance, must have an irrational function—intuition or sensation—to provide the thinking with an object. If one is a feeling type, and combines that with intuition, then there is an intuitive tone to the feeling. If feeling is instead combined with sensation, then the feeling responds mainly to objective facts. There is always the irrational background of the rational, or the rational background of the irrational.

The third function is more damaging, insofar as it is closer to the unconscious. It operates irregularly, so one doesn't have it always at hand. It requires a certain amount of effort to get it going. It doesn't flow by itself, and it creates a tension: intuition and thinking might be getting along okay, but the third function quarrels with them.

The ego, which is identified with the main two functions, can make a switch, but this is tiring and creates a certain amount of tension, though it is not necessarily a tragedy.

The fourth function, the inferior function, is different. It can only be assimilated by a complete change in the personality. And that is the death experience, because the inferior function is deeply incompatible with the main functions.

You can also say that in this fairy tale Dimitri *falls* into the cellar. He follows the horse along the way on which it will be well fed, but this leads to him being imprisoned. His activity has all the negative consequences of the inferior function without any of its redemptive aspects.

People sometimes confuse "going into the cellar" (drinking or sex orgies, etc.) with going into the unconscious. But the horse doesn't take him to the right place at all. There is a difference between just letting the animal instincts run wild, and exploring the unconscious. If there is no real sacrifice involved, there is only the cheap business of letting oneself go for the sake of it.

Another Siberian story concerned with the integration of the ancestors—related to going into the grandfather's cellar—is as follows:

A man named Wolf is called upon to get rid of a giant eagle who is killing the children of the community. Wolf sets out on his journey, crossing the plains until he comes to the mountain where the eagle lives. At the foot of this mountain he meets an old man and woman who greet him: "Oh, Wolf, have you come, grandchild? We knew you would come . . ."

They are his ancestors. They give him some talismans which

he takes with him and which aid him in the killing of the eagle. Then a huge round stone rolls out of the slain eagle. This is called "Rage of the Eagle," and it chases Wolf, threatening his life as he flees from it. He reaches the grave of his grandparents, jumps in, and hides, while the great stone rolls on by, now getting smaller and smaller until it is nothing but a pebble lying on the ground. And so it was that the ancestral spirits helped him.

In "The Virgin Czarina," after eating and drinking in his grandfather's cellar, Ivan comes to the Baba Yaga. This is a wonderful figure, a complete image of the Great Mother in both her positive and negative aspects. As soon as he refuses to answer her question—"Do you come here voluntarily or involuntarily?"—she feeds him. It is his attitude that determines what happens next.

You see, one of the great tricks of the mother complex in a man is always to implant doubt in his mind, suggesting that it might be better to do something else, this rather than that, and then the man is lamed; he gets lost in a fog of philosophical thinking instead of taking action. But Ivan says, "Shut up, you old witch! You shouldn't question a hero. Bring me something to eat and drink or I'll chop off your ears and knock off your head and sand will come out of your arse!" Whereupon the Baba Yaga cooks him a marvelous dinner and gives him good advice. She tries to make him infantile, but when she sees that he stands up to her, she turns positive and helps him.

The witch's hut stands on chicken legs (sometimes the story says cock's legs, with a cock's comb on the roof). The chicken represents a primitive, promiscuous, feminine Eros.

The hut rotates like a spindle. The only direct amplification of this is in Plato's *Timaeus*, where he represents the cosmos as a sphere surrounded by the world soul, which is divided into four parts. The whole thing rotates on an axis, a rotating spindle, spinning around in the womb of Nemesis (a goddess of justice or vengeance). The whole Platonic system turns around and around in her womb. Here the autonomous movement of nature is linked with the goddess of fate, who spins the thread of human life. The cocoon of fascinations and illusions which this figure spins makes up a man's life.

Spinning represents the aimless, circular movement of the psyche. An anima-possessed man goes spinning round and round the same experiences—he is in the cocoon of the goddess. He must say, as Ivan does to the spinning house: "Stop! Don't mill around—turn your back to me so I can go on."

There is a spinning of nature which leads nowhere if consciousness does not interrupt the movement of the unconscious. There is a spinning and milling around of symbols, a building up and tearing down in fantasies—a huge symbolic system building up, and then a breaking down. The ego must say, "Stop!" and straighten out this circular movement.

To a lesser degree, one sees this in people who are caught in a fate dictated by their unconscious. For instance, such a person may go through a series of marriages, all to the same type of man or woman. The spinning factor always creates the same fate. That is one of the witchy aspects of the unconscious.

"Child, do you come voluntarily, or involuntarily?"—that is a devilish question, raising eternal doubt. It is the riddle of the Sphinx, which the unconscious likes to bring in. Oedipus replied to the Sphinx that it is the human being, meaning that you must live it out. Or you can try another tactic, and say, "Shut up, you old witch! That is not a question for you to ask. You just run along now and bring me something to eat!"

That would be the primitive masculine attitude, which cuts out doubt and isn't vulnerable to insoluble conflict. It is better to take the attitude, "I know what I'm doing and I take responsibility for it." One of the Baba Yaga's tricks is to depotentiate the hero. In another version Ivan answers, "Shut up—I come voluntarily *and* involuntarily." Then she can't say anything more. It mirrors how this negative aspect can be stopped.

The Baba Yaga has a very long nose with which she scratches around in the stove. Witches often have a certain phallic aspect, a huge thumb or toe or nose, as here. The male in this primitive realm is just the phallus. That is why the Baba Yaga is so dangerous—she is everything, father and mother, male and female, symbols of totality and thus of the Self. But they represent a preconscious totality, the Uroborus, from which the male has to break free in order to live his authentic life.

This is especially the case with men in the first half of life: they have a certain preconscious totality which they cannot give up for fear of becoming one-sided. This is quite legitimate; what they have *is* completeness—but it is paradise behind instead of paradise ahead. Only the hero who has the courage to cut this totality off can find it again as a personal experience, not just as something given, inborn.

By cutting off the old witch, Ivan reaches Maria, the virgin czarina with the golden tresses. The three goddess-witches who thought to stop him end by giving him food and showing him the way. This is the pattern of how a man can break free from the devouring mother image and assimilate the feminine principle.

There is a collective aspect in this story: the Russian man has the typical problem of someone tied to the Earth Mother. He likes to drink tea and vodka and discuss doubts; he likes to start something, and then he gets lazy about carrying it through. There is no solution, no directedness by a disciplined consciousness. It is a trait typical of the puer aeternus.[21]

---

[21] [See von Franz, *The Problem of the Puer Aeternus;* also Daryl Sharp, *Digesting Jung: Food for the Journey,* pp. 99ff.—Ed.]

Of all the fairy tales I know, the Russian ones contain the most beautiful descriptions of this figure, who just mills about in the unconscious. That is perhaps why Communism is as it is today [1953], overdoing the perfectionist ideal, with any breaches of discipline being punished in harsh, exaggerated ways—by killing, imprisonment and so on. It is a compensation for their unconscious sloppiness.

Then Ivan jumps into a "fourth dimension" through the fourth witch, Maria, the virgin czarina. There may be a kinship connection here; we don't know this for sure, but it is a fair assumption, based on subsequent events, that Maria is indirectly connected with the three Baba Yagas.

Ivan comes to the Kingdom Under the Sun. Here the anima is combined with the sun and not with the moon. Only in the German and Russian languages is the sun designated as feminine and the moon masculine. In Russian, "Maria" is often the name of the sun. This feminizing of the sun and masculinizing of the moon is likely connected with the different makeup of these two nations, referring to fundamentally different attitudes. The sun generally represents the source of consciousness, while the moon is dimmer. Perhaps the main source of consciousness in Germany and Russia is in the unconscious. Their deepest thoughts and experiences come via inspiration, from the source of consciousness which paradoxically is in the unconscious. However, this is little more than speculation.

Ivan now comes to the castle and finds Maria, so beautifully transparent that he can see the marrow flowing in her bones. (In another version, she is not only transparent, but "her body one could encompass with two fingers, it is so small, but when one lets it go again, she fills the whole world.") She is the world soul and fills the whole cosmos. She is the soul of matter.

This figure appears in stories from the Caucasus way up to the far north—but always in Russia. These stories are a continuation of antique Greek Gnostic ideas which survived in these areas, although the Gnostics were aggressively persecuted in the Christian world. The Gnostics taught of a Sophia figure, a bride of God. In the tenth and eleventh centuries A.D., this goddess was described as the world soul who fills the whole cosmos.

This bride of God is His feminine aspect, which thus completes Him. The name Sophia means Wisdom. From the male God comes the wisdom found in the Bible in Revelation. But this goddess, this bride, reveals herself through experience—not through reading the Scriptures, but through experiencing the unknown, experiencing reality.

So we see that the tendency is toward assimilating this Sophia figure. This anima has the fantastic, antique character of a highly spiritualized world soul which, in the Western world, appears only in alchemy and in certain sects, but in the Eastern world survives in a more complete form.

Question: Could you say something more about the spinner and the spindle?

The Baba Yaga lives in a little house that rotates like a spindle. One cannot approach her unless one knows the magic verse: "Little hut, stand still, put your back away from me and the front toward me." This motif of the spindle, and of spinning in general, is always associated with goddesses of fate.

In India, it is Maya who spins the illusions of a person's life—the fascinations and attractions which entangle one. In Western tradition it is the Norns (the three Fates—past, present and future—who in Norse mythology live in the well at the foot of the mighty ash tree, Yggdrasil) or the three Greek fates (Clotho, Lachesis, Atropos, one of whom spun the thread of life, one who held it and fixed its length, and one who cut it off).

In the Platonic concept, it is the goddess Nemesis—a Great

Mother figure whose meaning is justice and vengeance—in whose womb resides the axis of the cosmos. Thus the mother goddess contains the spinning movement, whereas in our fairy tale she is inside, within the spindle.

Spinning certainly has to do with the movement of the unconscious psyche in general, and with the autonomous activities of the complexes in particular. We always try to interpret a dream as a compensation of the conscious situation. But besides this, it seems as if the unconscious is a living system which can move by itself. This is very difficult to prove, because one can always say that such and such has been called forth by the conscious ego. But we know from mythology that we must always reckon with arbitrary, autonomous events.

There is a parallel situation in modern physics, where we know now that there is a spontaneous, arbitrary movement in matter, movement which does not obey the law of causality and which cannot always be predicted. For example, you cannot predict when a particular uranium atom will fall apart. We do know the exact, definite number of years for uranium to become lead—that is, its "half-life," the length of time in which one-half of the atoms in a piece of uranium will have disintegrated and it will no longer be radioactive. But we still cannot answer the question, "How does each atom know when it is its turn?" Physicist can't predict just *which* atom will disintegrate.[22]

---

[22] ["The physical phenomenon of radioactivity consists in the transition of the atomic nucleus of the active substance from an unstable early state to its final state (in one or several steps), in the course of which the radioactivity finally stops. Similarly, the synchronistic phenomenon, on an archetypal foundation, accompanies the transition from an unstable state of consciousness into a new stable position .... The moments in time when the *individual* atoms disintegrate are in no way determined by the *laws of nature.*" (Letter 37, Pauli to Jung, in Wolfgang Pauli and C.G. Jung, *Atom and Archetype: The Pauli/Jung Letters,* p. 41)—Ed.]

So, if the material world has this possibility of spontaneous movement, why should the unconscious not have it too? This has to be taken into account: there is a development in the collective unconscious which cannot be explained as only an answer to consciousness. Probably there are the two systems, material and psychic, each affecting the other, both capable of spontaneous movement. The inner rotation is always linked with a symbol representing the deepest layers within the collective unconscious—where it somehow melds with the physical processes of the body, activating emotions.

Maria is walled away in her town. Hidden bells in the wall ring when the horse jumps over it and touches one of them. This brings about the movement of all the townspeople.

In practice, one sees this when dealing with women possessed by the witch archetype. Such women seem to have to stir up emotions purely for the sake of stirring them up, even if it is destructive. Such women, when they see a blind spot in one of their neighbors, just have to put their finger on it. They can't leave it alone. The witch anima in men has this tendency, too.

Normally, it is a shadow figure in women that has this trait, but in psychotic people it is sometimes an actual possession, and extremely destructive. A little bit of stirring up doesn't matter because sometimes having to talk about it can help bring out shadow elements which can then become conscious. So in a way it is positive, for it works toward clarity. But when it becomes autonomous, as happens in certain psychotic cases, then it can actually destroy people. You have the feeling with these psychotics that they do it just for the sake of having something destructive to do—an autonomous pleasure in keeping the devil going. They have a lust for destruction.

Baba Yaga is the feminine personification of a devil. Whoever approaches her hut faces dissolution, an eternal milling around.

But Ivan uses a magic incantation to change the situation. This shows that here we are dealing with elements of the unconscious which can only be affected by magic.

Sometimes a psychological content cannot be touched just by analyzing dreams. If we are up against such elements, something magical is needed. Then we are faced with the question: Do we have tools with which we can *do* something to the unconscious, not just bring it up into consciousness? The only means Jung has discovered up to now is active imagination. That is the only means by which *we* can have an effect on the unconscious. It is a technique of bewitching the unconscious, so to speak.[23] Some things cannot be assimilated just by making them conscious. A more active approach is required.

That is why Jung feels that if an analyst has to treat psychotics, he must know how to use active imagination for his own protection. A psychosis is a very infectious disease—it attacks from behind. One sees this happen often in a group, where half-psychotic, borderline personalities can stir everyone up. Wherever something in such a group is unconscious, then bang! they hit on it. The analyst needs to know how to disentangle himself from the psychotic effects of a patient. Otherwise, sooner or later he is caught, some day when he is tired, overworked or has fallen into his own black spots.

But there are other threats to the analyst besides psychic infection. He may be exposed to such terribly vile material from the unconscious of the patient that he himself is poisoned. The very fact that one has to listen to such things, or look at such drawings, has an affect on one's soul. That is why primitives are afraid to look at certain things. But, if one *has* to listen to or

---

[23] [See "The Transcendent Function," *The Structure and Dynamics of the Psyche*, CW 8; also Barbara Hannah, "On Active Imagination," in *The Inner Journey*, pp. 24ff.—Ed.]

look at such material, then there is a necessity to de-poison one-self, and active imagination is the most direct way to do so. Simply understanding is not enough.

Ivan instinctively knows what to do: with his magic verse he stops the hut from rotating, interferes with consciousness. In the Platonic image, the mother goddess is outside and the spinning wheel is inside, but here the spinning wheel has covered everything. There is nothing you can talk to, relate to. It is the most destructive abyss of feminine nature.

The witch is stirring the stove, that is, stirring up the emotions. The stove has to do with the stomach and intestines; that is where we cook food for assimilation. So the kitchen and the stove refer to everything that has to do with affect. The nucleus of the emotional psyche gets hit—then we have to run to the toilet, for example, to get rid of it.

Jung remarks on how the center of consciousness has risen up the body during the course of history. (He likes to say that dogs have their consciousness in their bladder, because they only think when they have to go out!) Among primitives the belief is common that the psyche is in the belly. Practically, only what affects their intestines exists as a psychological factor. They are not aware of anything more subtle than that, anything that does not hit their gut.

The Greeks thought the center of consciousness was in the diaphragm. Our word "schizophrenia" comes from that—"split diaphragm." Heracles, when in dire straits, talked to his diaphragm. Later, the heart was considered to be the center. Many Indian tribes "think with the heart," responding psychologically to factors which make the pulse beat faster. Still later the center moved to the breath: those factors that make us breathe irregularly are the only psychic contents we are aware of. Thus the center of consciousness moves up.

The stove always refers to the belly-psyche and those aware-
nesses connected with it. This type of witch must always make
an emotional fuss with her animus. She can't leave a situation to
develop on its own, but must drag everything into the light. That
is how witches are driven, always stirring up other people.

But Baba Yaga is not only scratching in the stove with her
nose. At the same time, she is combing yarn with her claws; that
is, she does make a certain order in life. Also she watches the
geese; that would be positive—she takes care of the instincts.
That is why, when Ivan talks to her in a certain brusque, masculine way—swearing at her most delightfully!—she becomes completely positive, becomes the goddess of fertility, feeding and
taking care of him.

The most striking thing about geese is that they are organized
in such a military fashion, wild geese always flying in chevron
formation, and tame geese always marching in single file. Animals have a pattern in their behavior. Geese let themselves be
invisibly organized. That is why the goose is the animal of the
goddess Nemesis, and of Aphrodite in her aspect as a mother
goddess. In the Chinese book of wisdom, the I Ching, hexagram
53 (nine at the top), says:

> The wild goose gradually draws near the cloud heights.
> Its feathers can be used for the sacred dance.
> Good fortune.[24]

The utmost fulfillment is that the human ritual follows the
order of the wild geese. There is this absolute harmony with nature; the greatest consciousness is like a return to the animal, but
on a higher level. The wild goose has to do with a secret order
within nature itself. That is why geese are associated with goddesses of fate.

---

[24] [Richard Wilhelm, trans., *The I Ching or Book of Changes,* p. 208.—Ed.]

Baba Yaga rules all the secret orders of nature; these drives are not chaotic, but follow a hidden pattern. However, in the figure of Maria, the virgin czarina with the golden tresses, the anima aspect comes out more.

The Kingdom Under the Sun contains the rejuvenating apples and the waters of life and death; that is, it is a sort of paradise, the Hesperides of the Greeks. *Hespera* means evening, when the sun sets, the end of the world. That is where Heracles went for the golden apples. So, Maria is the goddess of the setting sun, therefore actually a goddess of death, an aspect of the anima quite outside the human sphere, in the Beyond.

Maria is surrounded by the town wall. This again refers to ancient goddesses, most of whom were represented with the walls of the town as their crown—the familiar crenelated walls. There are certain quite interesting speculations about this during late antiquity, in which the goddess represents the world soul and the wall is matter which encloses it—her girdle or her crown is the outer part of her world soul. So the outer shell is the actual matter, and inside there is the symbolic, psychological fact.

This same representation is made on a higher scale. The *matter* of the cosmos—the anima in one of her deepest aspects—has to do with the actual secret of the world. How is the unconscious psyche linked with physical matter? That we don't know, though we do know there is a link. We can even compare this with the spinning—that would be the dynamic aspect of nature— and on the other side, matter has this mass aspect. Energy and substance are the two aspects of matter. We can look at matter as consisting of particles, or we can see it as magnetic fields.

The anima, Jung tells us, is "the archetype of life itself,"[25] and therefore she must have to do somehow with the actual physical

---

[25] ["Archetypes of the Collective Unconscious," *The Archetypes and the Collective Unconscius,* CW 9i, par. 66.—Ed.]

consistency of the cosmos, with the secret of world matter. She is dormant in it; she sleeps there. This physical aspect is only a shell; she is not matter, but she is inside the wall. From the psychological angle, we are observing the psyche with our consciousness, and then we may come to an element of the unconscious where we have the feeling, "That is no longer psychological, it is material"—the psychosomatic aspect. The two are linked; but we don't yet have the knowledge to know just how. And so, in working with the unconscious, we come to a border area of the psyche where it becomes somatic.

Physicists start from the other direction: they look at things pragmatically, and then they come to a borderline where the metaphysical (beyond their physical data) begins. The study of atomic physics makes it clear that we can no longer exclude the consciousness of the observer from the results of an experiment.

For example, all material phenomena can be studied either as waves of radiation, or as atomic particles. This is the great contradiction, that when we want to prove that light consists of particles, the only way we can do it is to move the light source. A screen is made with a little hole in it, and only one quantum of light is allowed to pass through; then only one molecule on the photographic plate is disintegrated. If you keep the light field static, you can say, "Now we know that light is all particles; the waves are an illusion." Then you move the light so that only one particle can move through, so there is no possibility of its shooting back and forth.

On the other hand, the wave theorists make a crystal screen and they break the light up. Then they get the phenomena of interference. When waves chase each other, they either get bigger or they level out, depending on how they hit each other. Wherever you have an interference pattern you get waves. So they say, "Light is waves, not particles." In order to create this phenomenon, the light source must be constant, and there must be a great amount of it.

Thus, in the first experiment, you cannot settle the time and space norms exactly, although the energy factor is exact—you can send off just one quantum of light, but time and space are the vague factors. In the second experiment, the amount of energy is the vague factor—it is not exactly measurable. The interesting conclusion is that it is the way in which the experiment is set up that determines the result. Whether we want to prove that light is waves, or that it is particles, we set up the experiment in such a way as to prove our hypothesis and to make it impossible to arrive at its opposite.

We have to do this in order to achieve a pure result; we have to corner nature, so to speak, have to ask a question in order to get an answer—but it ends all hope that we will ever be able to find out what matter really is. We can only say, "If we create this phenomenon with this hypothesis, nature will answer in this way; if we create this other phenomenon, nature will answer differently."

Therefore, the question one has in consciousness becomes a relevant factor: we have to include both the observer and the way the experiment is designed. When we want to find out one thing, we must sacrifice the other, either time-space exactness or the energy factor. We have to realize that in order to acquire one piece of knowledge, we have to sacrifice another; we cannot have it all. Moreover, we get results that are absolutely contradictory. So we are forced to acknowledge that under certain circumstances light can behave as either particles or waves, depending on how we design our research. We get two results which absolutely contradict each other.

What is interesting to us is the fact that people who have tried to study matter completely objectively have been forced back to psychology: the observer and the hypothesis in the observer's mind have to be included along with the external physical factors. In this way, scientists are discovering the reality of the unconscious. They started by working on the material aspect of nature and have proceeded to where they meet the borderline of the unconscious. The psychologist started working from the other side, from the unconscious, and now arrives at the borderline of the somatic, where the psyche seems to mirror itself in material facts.

It is a sign of our times that even in mathematics the same thing has happened. In what is called fundamental mathematics, it is recognized that even the basic axioms cannot be proved. Sensory experiences on the one side, and archetypal experiences in the psyche on the other, are the basis of mathematics as we know it today.

For example, take the axiom that "two parallels meet in infinity." That comes not only from visual experience, where two parallel lines meet in the far distance, but also from certain inherent laws of the mind—and hanging in mid-air between these two experiences is mathematics.

And so the whole of natural science has shifted over to being a description; that is, if you look at such and such this way, then you get these results, and if you look at such and such in another way, then you get these other results. Both the observer and the inherent activity of the human mind have to be taken into account. Natural science has the advantage of being able to measure its phenomena to a certain extent, and to demonstrate results which are statistically true. Its experiments can be repeated exactly, over and over again, and are not too dependent on the subjective factor. But this is only true in microphysics. As soon as you deal with millions of atoms, then you get laws which are only relatively true, only average reactions.

In the study of the unconscious, it is the archetypes that are the fundamental factors. Their activity is the only thing you can predict with a degree of certainty. Case material is always strictly individual, which is why we say that theory must take a back seat when dealing with a particular person in a given life situation.

In our tale, Ivan goes over the wall and comes to something beyond, which we can call psychic reality, based on the hypothesis that the psyche is in itself absolutely real. (Of course, we have to have a name for the unknown stuff we are studying, so we call it "the unconscious.") Ivan comes to this reality of matter, and there he finds Maria asleep. When he turns away after raping her, she wakes up.

So, Maria lives in a counter-movement to Ivan's rhythm. Similarly, we can say that when our ego consciousness is focused, then we cannot be aware of the unconscious. And to be aware of the unconscious, our consciousness has to be dimmed. The best phenomena of this sort are dreams, where consciousness is just barely awake, but not enough to interfere with what is going on in the unconscious. The dream arises at the borderline between consciousness and the unconscious.

The concept of "highest consciousness" is where we disagree with traditional Eastern philosophers. They say that *samadhi* is the highest state of consciousness, whereby absolute reality is the complete dimming out, the extinction, of the ego. Jung argues that this state represents total unconsciousness, but in the East it is considered to be the highest level of consciousness. So, there are these two complementary qualities: you cannot be conscious and unconscious at the same time. Active imagination is an attempt to keep the ego intact and at the same time bring the borderline phenomena of dreams into it. That is why it is the recommended technique for bringing together the opposites.

Understanding the meaning of a dream also requires a dimming down of consciousness. The Eastern way would mean the giving up of ego consciousness, and in the West we do not consider that to be a good idea because then we lose the possibility of scientific description. For instance, when Jung was in African bush country he determined to observe the natives' psychic phenomena scientifically, with careful notes and records. Then he had some of their experiences, but when he looked at his notes later, he told me that they were completely lacking!

So it is, if you keep the scientific mind, you walk through the bush and don't have the experiences—nothing happens. And if you go through the bush as the natives do, then the light of ego consciousness is extinguished and you are unable to take scientific notes. It is our consciousness which distinguishes between the outside and the inside. If our consciousness is extinguished, there is no longer that distinction—everything is simply an *event,* with the inner phenomena actually occurring outside.

A friend told me of a missionary who once sat all night beside a medicine man, who before falling into a trance had said that he was going to a mountain far away to meet other medicine men— a sort of ghost meeting. The missionary asked the medicine man if along the way he might deliver a message to a friend living in that mountain area: "Please return my rifles." Some days later the missionary received a letter from his friend saying that he had been wakened on the night of the trance by a voice outside saying, "Please return my rifles."

I think such a thing can only happen if you are in a trance or otherwise unconscious—then what is happening inside can manifest outside. We often feel that way about dreams, but we know the difference when we wake up. The medicine man's communication can be seen as a manifestation of the unconscious in a time and space that is not accessible to consciousness. That is not by any means an unheard-of phenomenon. But you who are watching are excluded from going to the mountain. These are complementary qualities or abilities: you can either have the experience or you can keep a scientific account of it—you cannot do both.

In "The Virgin Czarina," Maria is transparent. In the parallel story it is said that she could be picked up between two fingers, but at the same time fills the whole world. Obviously she has a subtle body, with no density; she doesn't have the qualities of ordinary matter. Transparency also refers to the ghost world—you can put your hand through ghosts but not touch them. Ivan could see the marrow flowing through her bones; that is, she was also a skeleton. In some stories the anima figure appears as a beautiful woman from the front, but when she turns her back she is a skeleton, death. This aspect was in the story about the star goddess, who also was a dancing skeleton.[26]

The star-maiden's home was a misty dominion, and here we have Maria living on the borderline between life and death. This makes her a supernatural being. She is not material. Her body is like a shell which you can look through. Ivan rapes this figure in her sleep, and then he runs away. She wakes up when his horse touches the bell. When Ivan went in, his horse didn't touch it, but going out he was in such a rush that he set off the alarm.

This motif of touching was also in the story where the girl rides successively through the brass, silver and gold forests, and is told by the blue bull not to touch the leaves or the troll would emerge.[27] In that story, the leaves signified the mortal side of experience. In the present story, the wall is where the physical quality is touched, where the thing becomes real. That is the danger point, for the anima is from the spiritual realm, not a concrete woman.

---

[26] [See above, pp. 65f.—Ed.]
[27] [See above, pp. 51f.—Ed.]

The image of the anima must be realized as a psychological entity—but there is the human experience, too, and there is always a hook of some sort; otherwise, why would the man be attracted to this particular, real woman? When the anima is linked with a human being, that is when it becomes a challenge in a man's life.

This happens not only in connection with the anima—it happens whenever a dream speaks to us, and we ask ourselves: "Must I deal with this concretely or symbolically?" It is a very difficult problem, one of the most ethically demanding points of the whole analytic process.

In general, if one has the patience to wait long enough, one learns from the dream whether it wants to be realized in fact or symbolically. But very often there are dreams where you just don't know; you must try one way, and then another. If you have not taken the right course, the dream will insist on correcting you.

Here Ivan touches the bell—there is a vibration going through him, an emotional reaction. One of the main qualities of archetypal symbols is that they have an enormous load of energy; they are explosive factors. Therefore they are responsible for dynamic movements like Nazism, for instance, and for what goes on in the insane.

Archetypes release the most overwhelming emotions. The image and the emotion are the two factors we are aware of, but what is behind them we don't know; that is, we don't know what the archetype is in itself. We know only that it occurs repeatedly as a similar picture or pattern, and we know that it has this enormous, dynamic effect in the moment when it touches the edge of the physical being. The archetype has to do with the instinct; the instinct has to do with physical activity. The archetype is a common way of experiencing things in a psychological manner. It is linked with the instinct; it is the pattern of the instinct. When it is realized instinctively, that is when the emotion arises.

People sometimes have an archetypal dream and experience no other effect than to think, "All this mythology is very interesting." This isn't necessarily because the analyst hasn't been able to convey its significance. It may be just that it is too far removed. But it can happen that even a year later the patient feels a tremendous emotion and comes running in a panic to the analyst—because now it has come through! Now they understand, whereas previously the archetype was unapproachable. This borderline, where the physical and the psychological meet, is what rings a bell and causes the internal vibration.

We know the Eastern image of the Kundalini as a dormant snake. The Yogi concentrates and makes her rise, and the first thing is that a gong sounds—that is the awakening of the Kundalini. That is what we mean when we say that something is "constellated." This wonderful word comes from astrology and astronomy, where one says that the stars have moved into a certain constellation. It is also a most mysterious word. What does it mean that something is suddenly constellated? It is a wonderful word to cover up what we don't really know! It is the moment of touching human reality. Before, it slept as a possibility within the human being. That is why this is also the borderline between life and death—it is dormant, not yet real.

Ivan's horse—its left hind foot—touches the bell, makes the fatally hopeful mistake. It is like the sin in Paradise, a *felix culpa,* a fortunate crime by which a step forward in consciousness is made. Every step in consciousness is always seen as a fatal mistake, a violation of nature. That is why a person who is "too sound," like certain simple peasants who live in a harmonious relatedness to nature, may have all the archetypes in them, but they are not constellated; they exist in their life, but they are dormant. You can't talk with them about such things because they are not constellated as a reality. Consciousness must first be split off, which causes some emotional disturbances, but then one can realize the inner nature.

The animal impulsiveness of Ivan does this—drags the left hind foot a little—a tendency to the Dimitri side. But that constellates the possibility of realization. Maria then puts wings on herself and on all her servants, and thus reveals her ghost nature, her spiritual nature, in response to the fact that Ivan has touched the physical. This brings forth the other aspect: she was dormant, and he has now brought about this counter-movement.

What rings a bell touches a complex; it hits the inner life. At that very moment Ivan receives the most terrific fright. Maria is after him! That is a typical representation of dealing with the anima when consciousness isn't yet strong enough to relate to her. Perhaps this story reveals the Russian problem: he can rape the anima only when she is asleep. When she wakes up, he is terrified. This terror is a symbol of a weak consciousness.

The three Baba Yagas slow down the anima, inviting her in for tea and so on. With all this stopping and talking, Maria is delayed. (This is also an image of what the Russians do: when they are frightened—they delay the problem so that it can't become really crucial.) This "old-woman talk" is sometimes very helpful, for it protects against a realization that consciousness is not ready for. The mother figures become like a buffer between consciousness and the awareness of the anima. This is represented here as positive, but the need for the mothers to help, to interfere, highlights a typical problem in Russian psychology.

Ivan returns to the court, and apparently nothing has happened to him. His brother takes the golden apples and the water of life and death, and goes boasting to the court that he was the one who found them. Ivan doesn't even try to disprove this. He just goes off and gets drunk again. It looks as if nothing has changed.

That again is a reflection of the Russian soul. They have the greatest inner experiences, but when it comes to living life in this world, the old, eternal way takes over again. The creative gifts dormant in their psyche are of the greatest value, but they regard them with a primitive awe, so they get lost and not used.

Ivan simply does not trouble himself about the matter. Again, this is an effect of the mother complex, which always sweeps away what has been gained. This is the puzzling thing about the Russians, who we know have really been confronted with serious religious challenges, as revealed for example in Dostoyevsky's *The Brothers Karamazov.* This problem is probably connected with the sun's being linked to the anima: the possibilities of con-sciousness are still in the unconscious. Experiences are received as inspiration only, and do not become a quality of ego con-sciousness—the ego *receives* the experience, remaining in the passive state.

In *Psychology and Alchemy,* Jung tells of a man who dreamed that an unknown woman—the anima—was worshipping the sun, which means that the whole spiritual genius of this man is still in the unconscious, still linked to the animal realm.[28] Such people can make great discoveries, but only because they arise from the unconscious. They haven't worked things out themselves, they just came into their head. New data that is not consciously ac-quired can easily become lost again. It is just a gift from the an-ima, and it can fall back into the unconscious.

At this point in the fairy tale, everything seems to be lost. Dimitri, who is doing the boasting, has actually only been in the

---

[28] [CW 12, par. 110.—Ed.]

cellar of the woman with the turning bed. She can be compared with the Greek goddess Circe, who touched with her wand every man who came to her island and made them all into pigs—that is, blinded them with instinct. And now it is Dimitri who takes over and says, "I'm the one who had the experience." But the real mystic experience is denied in the unconscious.

This is like the situations where people have tremendous experiences during analysis, but then have great difficulty in bringing them into their real life. They ask, "So, what shall I do now?"—and the experience is all gone. One can have a wonderful analysis, but in the conscious field nothing moves. It was like taking a bath: one feels clean, but nothing has really changed.

The technical term for this in mythology is "difficulty on the return." The hero has overcome great obstacles, slain the dragon, etc., but on the way back he either falls asleep and everything is lost again, or the treasure is taken from him, as in the Gilgamesh Epic, where a snake steals the elixir of life from Gilgamesh as he takes a swim. It seems to be just as great an achievement to make the transition back, to reconnect with outer life, as it is to brave the unconscious in the first place. But if it isn't accomplished, then the whole business is like an intoxication. One wakes up with a hangover, and afterward everything is as it was before.

That is why Jung is against hypnosis—insight does not last unless it is done step by step, really consolidated in consciousness.[29] In the long run, quick techniques do not work because the

---

[29] [Jung: "I did not give up hypnosis because I wanted to avoid dealing with the basic forces of the human psyche, but because I wanted to battle with them directly and openly. When once I understand what kind of forces play a part in hypnotism I gave it up, simply to get rid of all the indirect advantages of this method." ("Crucial Points in Psychoanalysis," *Freud and Psychoanalysis,* CW 4, par. 601)—Ed.]

unconscious and the ego have not really been linked.

For Ivan, the difficult achievement of bringing his experiences into consciousness is too much: when he returns to the court, he forgets all about them. He takes up his old way of life, and what he learned on his journey seems to be lost.

This danger of losing everything is illustrated in another story of a man who wins and marries a princess in another realm, but after a while wants to go back to his old home for a visit. The princess is very anxious about this, and says, "Don't forget me, and whatever you do, don't kiss your mother!" He promises, but once back in his old home he forgets and does kiss his mother. Immediately he loses all memory of his experience with the princess.

It is often tempting to dismiss an important experience by giving a reductive interpretation, saying, "Oh, that was nothing but . . ." The devil gets in and interprets something that you haven't experienced in exactly that way, and then all is lost. That is always the difficulty faced by consciousness—to link the two worlds, to realize both the inner and the outer aspects of what happens in one's life.

But here it is not true that everything is lost, because Maria is pregnant, and Ivan is the father of the two boys. Only *apparently* is everything lost. Something which has once happened is never lost forever. Whatever has been constellated has been moved in the unconscious itself, and the experience is still there somewhere. The psychic moment has been activated; the anima is impregnated by the fact that Ivan has been there. The two boys growing up give the ego enough strength to allow an irruption of unconscious material into consciousness.

Maria appears, firing guns, threatening to destroy the whole town if the father of her two sons doesn't show himself. She brings the same brutal force as Ivan had when he entered her town and raped her. This reflects the current state of Russian culture, where an overenlightened attitude admits of nothing irrational; everything is seen through the lens of nineteenth-century mechanistic materialism, which we in the West have rejected. That is raping Maria. Thus there is a very brutal counter-attack—suddenly the unconscious fights back. Older cultures have a more balanced relationship with life; there is always a movement and a counter-movement, but they don't take this violent form.

Shooting with guns symbolizes very strong emotions. An explosion initiates the attack. It truly feels as if one has been shot in the back. So, shooting is an emotional approach—it means being charged, loaded. That is what the anima, Maria, now does. She just shoots down the world of consciousness. This is the dangerous thing about sudden, undisciplined emotions. They can overrun reason, make people go berserk. Then the whole conscious program is shot down. That is Maria's revenge for having been raped by Ivan.

The king's court must find out what has happened. After trying some wrong solutions, like putting forward the older brothers as the father of the twins, they resort to Ivan. The anima is then satisfied, and the czar at last recognizes Ivan as the one who followed in his footsteps. He offers Ivan his kingdom, but Ivan says, "No thanks," and goes off with Maria into the Kingdom Under the Sun, which means that the whole thing goes back into the unconscious. From a psychological point of view it is not a happy ending. In spite of the richness and creativity in the unconscious, you often find that the conscious town is destroyed.

Among other peoples, similar stories relate that the czar keeps half the kingdom and gives the other half to his son and bride. So, even from the standpoint of the collective, this story has a sad end. The greatest values still disappear into the unconscious, which means that the possibility of becoming conscious is pretty small. Before, in this story we had a male world and a female world. The end result is still completely unconscious, but at least there has been a shift toward a greater balancing of the opposites. So we can say that if it continues to happen, over and over, then one day a balance may come about.

People fall again and again into the same hole; they will seem to have gained a little ground, but then they fall in again. This goes on repeatedly—but there is always a little bit of the hole filled in, a few of the gains retained. When they next fall into the trap, there is the feeling, "Oh! I've been here before, and I managed to get out."

Each time one gains a little ground, becomes a bit more conscious, it is a sort of secret confirmation of the personality. And so a little change has indeed occurred, but it is not the end of the story.

Bibliography

General

Edinger, Edward F. *The Aion Lectures: Exploring the Self in Jung's Aion.* Toronto: Inner City Books, 1996.

_____. *Goethe's Faust: Notes for a Jungian Commentary.* Toronto: Inner City Books, 1984.

Grimm Brothers. *The Complete Grimm's Fairy Tales.* New York: Pantheon Books, 1972.

Hannah, Barbara. *The Inner Journey: Lectures and Essays.* Toronto: Inner City Books, 2000.

Jung, C.G. *The Collected Works* (Bollingen Series XX). 20 vols. Trans. R.F.C. Hull. Ed. H. Read, M. Fordham, G. Adler, Wm. McGuire. Princeton: Princeton University Press, 1953-1979.

Olesch, Reinhold, ed. *Russian Folktales.* Trans. E.C. Elstob and Richard Barber (from the German edition; Dusseldorf: Eugen Diederichs Verlag, 1959). London: G. Bell & Sons, 1971.

Pauli, Wolfgang, and Jung, C.G. *Atom and Archetype: The Pauli/Jung Letters 1932 - 1958.* Ed. C.A. Meier (with the assistance of C.P. Enz and M. Fierz). Tr. David Roscoe. Introductory essay by Beverly Zabriskie. Princeton: Princeton University Press, 2001.

Sharp, Daryl. *Digesting Jung: Food for the Journey.* Toronto: Inner City Books, 2001.

_____. *Personality Types: Jung's Model of Typology.* Toronto: Inner City Books, 1987.

von Beit, Hedwig. *Symbolik des Märchen.* 3 vols. Jena, Germany: Eugene Diederichs Verlag, 1923.

von Franz, Marie-Louise. *Alchemy: An Introduction to the Symbolism and the Psychology.* Toronto: Inner City Books, 1980.

_____. *Apuleius' Golden Ass.* Zürich: Spring Publications, 1970.

_____. *Archetypal Patterns in Fairy Tales.* Toronto: Inner City Books, 1997.

_____. *Aurora Consurgens: On the Problem of Opposites in Alchemy.* Toronto: Inner City Books, 2000.

122

_____. *C.G. Jung: His Myth in Our Time.* Toronto: Inner City Books, 1998.

_____. *The Cat: A Tale of Feminine Redemption.* Toronto: Inner City Books, 1999.

_____. *On Divination and Synchronicity: The Psychology of Meaningful Chance.* Toronto: Inner City Books, 1980.

_____. *The Problem of the Puer Aeternus.* Toronto: Inner City Books, 2000.

_____. *Redemption Motifs in Fairy Tales.* Toronto: Inner City Books, 1980

_____. *Shadow and Evil in Fairy Tales.* Zürich: Spring Publications, 1974.

von Franz, Marie-Louise, and Hillman, James. *Lectures on Jung's Typology.* Zürich: Spring Publications, 1971.

Wilhelm, Richard, trans. *The I Ching or Book of Changes.* London: Routledge and Kegan Paul, 1968.

On Animus and Anima

Hannah, Barbara. "The Problem of Contact with Animus," and "The Religious Function of the Animus in the Book of Tobit." In *The Inner Journey: Lectures and Essays on Jungian Psychology.* Ed. Dean L. Frantz. Toronto: Inner City Books, 2000.

Jung, C.G. "Anima and Animus." In *Two Essays on Analytical Psychology,* CW 7, pars. 296-340.

_____. "Animus and Anima." In *Alchemical Studies,* CW 13, pars. 57-63.

_____. "Concerning the Archetypes, with Special Reference to the Anima Concept." In *The Archetypes and the Collective Unconscious,* CW 9I, pars. 111-147.

_____. "The Syzygy: Anima and Animus." In *Aion,* CW 9ii, pars. 20-42.

Jung, Emma. *Animus and Anima.* Zurich: Spring Publications, 1957.

Index